MAHAVATAR BABAJI SPEAKS

SHIFTING CONSCIOUSNESS TO FIFTH DIMENSION

AshaShri

INDIA • SINGAPORE • MALAYSIA

ISBN
Paperback 979-8-89632-771-4
Hardcase 979-8-89777-293-3

CONTENTS

एकं एव द्वितीयं
एको देवाः सर्व भूतान्तरात्मा
एक भाषा भूतकरुण्य रूप
एकम् लक्ष्यम् समारस्यम् समेशम्
एकम सर्वम चित्तमानंद पूर्णम

Ekam eva dwitiyam
Eko Deva: Sarva Bhutantartama
Ek Baasha Bhootakarunya Roop
Ekam Lakshyam Samarasyam Samesham
Ekam Sarvam Chittamananda Purnam

FOREWORD

सर्वस्व अर्पण करूं महावतार बाबा को,
सिद्ध करूं प्रणाम, मृत्युंजय बाबाजी का ले
कल्याणकारी नाम

Sarvasva Arpan karun Mahavatar
Baba ko, Siddhan Karun Pranam,
Mrityunjay Babaji ka Le kalyankari Naam

"*Mahavatar Babaji Speaks*" book is written by Brahmavidvamani Dr. Asha Gupta whose pen name is Asha Shri. This book is dedicated to all the soul brothers and sisters who are ready to walk the path of spirituality in this birth. This book contains all the wisdom spoken by Babaji to Asha Shri's consciousness, along with time period details.

When Asha Ji looked back on her fifteen years of this life journey with Mahavatar Babaji, she was overwhelmed with the realization that, all of her experiences were guide towards the ascension of human consciousness. With the intention of evolution of Earth consciousness, Babaji himself guided Asha to raise the energies of the planet and take it towards the fifth dimension. I also had many miraculous meditation experiences; Babaji has chosen us for a great purpose.

This book has been designed for the complete development of body, mind and soul of every consciousness present on Earth. The book, *"Mahavatar Babaji Speaks"*, which reflects the miraculous and eternal Divine Love of Mahavatar Babaji. It is a passport of Earth, as well as every consciousness present in Earth, which are ready to ascend into the fifth dimension.

We transcend and keep raising our consciousness, if we choose to. I hope, all of us will be able to shift into the fifth dimension. We are all multidimensional beings with the potential to access higher dimensions... Higher state of consciousness. We can heal ourselves now than ever before faster because of this higher consciousness. During this period, every human consciousness can connect, see and receive messages by being into their self-aware state.

Once we shift into the fifth dimension, we will feel that great powers have come within us. This book will give its readers a complete wisdom of Babaji's guidance towards entering into the fifth dimension and attaining higher frequencies and energies. Discovering the soul's path to heal itself by knowing. It is awakening to the fifth dimension. This dimension is pure love, pure light, unconditional forgiveness and acceptance.

Our soul despite of being with Gurus and Masters and having experiences with them, despite being in contact with them, through them, despite listening to Babaji's words, even in their presence, we are still in that moment of our life, given by the Masters, moving forward into our divinity. This is the divinity that Babaji has always spoken about. Divinity is the right of every human being. Divinity is part of us, within us and it is who we are.

We should spend every moment living it. Remembering this, every moment will change our thoughts. As our thoughts change, our mental body will change. All our reasons will end. All our actions will change. We will come to a royal path and start walking on such a path that no one would have experienced the joy derived from it till date. The energy with which Babaji has connected us today is about the golden future. May this book open a door for you, a portal into the fifth dimension which is a way of thinking and living.

I feel immensely fortunate to present to you the many experiences of AshaShri's. I feel blessed to be a witness of many of these physical form experiences as well as a listener of Mahavatar Babaji's messages through Asha.

With Love

Arun Kumar Gupta
Founder
Asha Foundation

PREFACE

गुरु मध्ये स्थितम् विश्वम,
विश्व मध्ये स्थितो गुरुः,
गुरु विश्वम् नमस्तेस्तु,
विश्वगुरू नमभ्यहम्

Guru madhye sthitam Vishwam,
Vishwa madhye sthito Guruh,
Guru Viswam Namastestu,
Vishwaguru Namabhyaham

Golden doors for Yoga Sadhana has opened for first time when Yogavatar Lahiri Mahasaya has given stress on use of Kriya Yoga in behavioral aspects of human beings as Guru. A golden bridge is created through which each and every human irrespective of their gender, class, creed and also being in their physical lives of family and responsibilities can cross and attain awakening, realization of self, Aham Brahmasmi and realizes death as the new beginning. This passport has been provided by Mahavatar Babaji, the guide and aspiration of thousands of seekers all over the world. Babaji also known as Kriya Babaji Nagraj, Mahavatar

Babaji, Shiv Baba and Mahamuni Babaji. To help humanity for the shift of consciousness, to evolve and attain enlightenment. Babaji has come in different forms whenever needed according to divine plan of ShivShakti. Babaji can take any physical form anytime and anywhere.

There are many great seekers in our spiritual history who have been very lucky to witness Babaji and understand his divine teachings with their extra sensory perceptions i.e. clairaudience, clairvoyance, clairsentience and claircognizance. I was one among such fortunate souls. With God's grace and Guru's blessings, I have received the immense pleasure of many witnesses of Babaji in this birth. I had seen Babaji energies many times in physical forms and also in the physical bodies of others.

There are many stages in meditation of different consciousness. We should believe in our deep knowledge and analytical power to experience these stages. We should not be afraid of our thoughts and experiences. This state strengthens with continuous practice and devotion. We may receive Babaji's guidance. In Paramahansa Yogananda's book, *"Autobiography of a Yogi"*, we can see Babaji's allusion as a great Master in spirituality. Babaji appears to be a youth of around 25 years.

Through this book *"Mahavatar Babaji Speaks"*, we will explore spirituality and reconnect with our heritage. Many saints and yogis have evolved in the history of India. They have always enlightened the lives on earth with their divine light. These great Masters have also shown us the way to live with spirituality.

Attaining spiritual satisfaction and awakening had been a challenging task in this materialistic world. To find out a solution to this challenge zeitgeist Mahavatar Babaji has given us the wisdom of Kriya Yoga which was also explained in Geeta by Lord Krishna and in the Yoga Sutras by Rishi Patanjali. He took the responsibility of spreading the teachings of Kriya Yoga, 5000 years old which was almost forgotten by the world.

Under this project, Babaji have been providing guidance to many Masters in physical and non-physical forms. For example, Adi Shankaracharya Ji (788 AD–820 AD), Kabirdas Ji (1407–1518), Lahiri Mahasaya Ji (1828–1895), Shri Yukteshwar Giri Ji (1855–1936) and Paramahansa Yogananda Ji (1893–1952). At the age of 16 itself, Babaji attained the highest state of Enlightenment.

Babaji has also been giving guidance about the transition of Earth from third to fifth dimension and for this, I am the fortunate chosen one. Dedicating this work from my heart, let us proceed friends. I accepted the work given to me wholeheartedly and started working on it. And it is going to be accomplished with Babaji's blessings.

Babaji's arrival in my life was like spring knocking at my door. With his divine presence, sight and experiences Babaji helped me to learn and understand this knowledge and helped to activate extra senses in human beings. Dedicated meditation practice for awakening of crystalline consciousness and welfare of humanity helps to receive Babaji's blessing. Experiencing these divine acquaintances is the greatest gift of human life.

My magical experiences with Mahavatar Babaji have been beautifully and sincerely put down by my own expression of love and light for you dear readers. I tried my level best to deliver Babaji messages.

I express my deep gratitude to Brahmarishi Patri Sir, who has shown us the path of Meditation. Meditation is a Yoga practice which helps us to release all past emotions which are deep rooted within us. It helps to overcome our desires and enhance our divinity. Meditation process helps us to make our mind stable and move on the path of self -attainment.

I am thankful to Dr. Shikha Tyagi, Dr. Ridhi Bakshi, Divya K and Oshin Agarwal for their hard work for this Great book. I am thankful to Notion Team for their support for patiently long waiting for the manuscript and working on it. I am sending lots of love to dear Snigdha Goel for gifting me Mahavatar Babaji's Painting as per my request. Our book cover page is this painting only. Babaji painting elicits an emotional response. I felt love, connection and surrender. I choose it as cover of *"Mahavatar Babaji Speaks"*.

Dear Readers, seekers and Kriya yogis, I know you are very excited to hold this magical book in your hands. Babaji asked me to produce a movie but due to some reasons I was not able to make it. So, I requested Babaji, *"Instead of a movie, can I write a book on you", he agreed and said "Through this book, the whole world will know that you are my child."* That's how I am presenting this book to you.

The language used in this book is simply communicating English through which I tried to express my genuine emotions at a particular event. My shared experiences are all true as they are explicitly cited in the book.

When I was combining all my experiences in 2022, I was surprised to realize that this was the wisdom of shift towards the fifth dimension given by Babaji for whole humanity. It is important for the spiritual attainment of all the souls on earth who are ready for the full soul integration. There are many events in this book which are shared experiences of my husband and spiritual friend Shri Arun Kumar Gupta Ji and my daughter Devika Gupta. We are a spiritual family, and the group energy that forms during a meditation session always brings us new experiences with Babaji and the Masters.

I am only a medium for making this wisdom available for this humanity. With the hope that you will also be able to feel immense dedication for Babaji and will progress on the way of ascension in your present lives.

Shifting our Consciousness to the Fifth Dimension, signifies a change of Era, a higher vibrational state, a vigilant society, where awakened individually and Enlightened beings live their divine lives.

With the message of Vasudeva Kutumbakam, I present this book for all spiritual seekers with all faith and love and light.

Thank you Babaji!

AshaShri

INTRODUCTION

We all live in a galaxy called the *'Milky Way'*. There are forty-eight dimensions in this entire universe.

The bottom one to twelve dimensions are what we call the Lower Heavenly Worlds and the top thirteen are what we call the Higher Heavenly Worlds. Beyond thirteen, there is a gate in between, which is called Lyra Star Gate and this gate is near the twelfth dimension. A clear picture of this was shown to me by Babaji in meditation. Mahavatar Babaji had shown me the reason for coming to earth.

161 years ago, the light of enlightenment, knowledge of Brahma and Kriya Yoga emerged from the caves of the Himalayas and spread across the world. This supreme knowledge of liberation of the soul has been spread in all the countries by Mahavatar Babaji's disciple Lahiri Mahasaya Ji and by other gurus in the Kriya Yoga tradition

like Shri Yukteswar Giri Maharaj, Shri Bhupendra Nath Sanyal, Shri Paramahansa Yogananda Ji, Shri Paramahansa Satyananda Giri Ji. This knowledge is moving forward on earth through Shri Paramahamsa Hariharananda Giri Ji, Swami Satyeswarananda Giri Ji and many other Gurus and is still growing.

Mahavatar Babaji helped those Mumukshu's and also had direct contact with them, so that they could experience direct personal contact with God and pave the way for their spiritual progress as fast as possible and show a new direction to this world. I always had a thought that while living in a household, Babaji gave me such experiences through meditation and such an easy meditation, Anapanasati meditation.

In the thirty-third year of Lahari Mahasaya Ji's life, the purpose of his life was fulfilled for which he was born on this earth. The specialty of Yogiraj Ji's initiation was that, not only did he get initiated, but all his disciples who chose this path of sadhana also got initiated. This chain kept moving forward. This incident did not happen only with Lahri Mahasaya Ji but it was a very sacred moment for the entire human race.

The supreme knowledge of Yoga, which had become extinct and remained unknown for a long time, came to light again on which Mother Ganga descended from heaven to earth and satisfied the devotee Bhagiratha with her Ganga water. Similarly, this great divine and wonderful stream of Kriya Yoga came out of the caves of the Himalayas and started moving towards the noisy life of man and the noisy settlements and started satiating everyone's hunger. The reason and the only reason were that the time had come for the Earth to shift to the fifth dimension.

I was talking about the dimensions of the Earth. The Earth once shone brightly at a place where Earth was known as '*Tara*'. But gradually malice, deception and deceit came into human consciousness and people even forgot their divine form. Forgetting brotherhood and getting trapped in the conflict of life, made life full of difficulties and transferred this low energy to earth. Babaji connects with many divine consciousness among which I was also one. When Babaji met me for the first time, he gave me an experience. I clearly saw that the Lyra Star Gate was opening and thousands of people following me and crossing the Lyra Star Gate. I was able to receive Babaji's knowledge on spirituality.

I was becoming a medium to impart spiritual activities and spiritual science to millions of consciousnesses. Thousands of people are going near the Lyra Gate. The earth will again find its lost divinity. On earth, many such consciousnesses are being born and will be born and are changing and developing themselves even in a life full of human challenges and conflicts. Through sadhana, meditation, yoga and Kriya Yoga, human beings can recognise their divinity even while doing all kinds of activities in their everyday life. New consciousnesses will be formed as new children on earth are born with advanced consciousness. In this way the consciousness of the earth will be born and transformed.

What a task have been given to us to bring about this change on Earth? Yoga Avatar had declared that God is possible only through the realisation of self-enlightenment. Those who cannot believe in the divinity of any human being will now be able to see their complete divinity by adopting this meditation practice.

By the end of this book, I will explain to you in simple and detailed language, about Kriya Yoga. The whole world got information about Kriya Yoga, for the first time in 1946, through Paramahansa Yogananda's book *'Yogi Kathaamrit'*. Since then, this Yoga has been continuously given to the world in Western countries, in America, all over the world through the great incarnation of the East.

This light that has ignited in the world was clearly explained by Yogi Lahiri Mahasaya Ji. Before he was leaving his body, Yogavatar said, *"I am leaving after establishing this immortal light that I have received from the closeness of Gurudev on earth. This knowledge of meditation will be discussed in every home. Human beings will move forward on the path of liberation."*

We are so lucky to witness the auspicious moment when Mahavatar Babaji brought the Ganga of knowledge on this earth and this Ganga is still flowing in this world through his loyal disciples. The entire world is being illuminated by the divine knowledge of yoga ignited by Mahavatar Babaji.

For all those who are curious to know themselves, for meditators and for every seeker following the path of Kriya Yoga, this book will present such a kind of energy which will enable the receptive seeker to ways, and put techniques meditation, teachings and knowledge given by the Guru and will be able to assimilate the knowledge.

The knowledge which was given by Lord Shri Krishna to Arjun in Bhagwat Geeta about the imperishable ancient Brahma Yoga Vidya, to which Lord Krishna said that I have provided this Vinay Sheel Yoga to the Sun God, Vivasvana and he has given this knowledge to Manu. Manu has transferred it to Iksvaku. In this sequence, this secret reached the sages and after that it disappeared for some time. Again, this wisdom is being given to this world by Babaji.

Here, we see this situation of the earth where the era has changed. I saw the word *"MEDITATION"* in the sky in 2010. This Meditation came into my life through Babaji. In this way, as per the need of time on earth, Babaji appeared in my consciousness and told me how to work with the emotional body, physical body and the spiritual causal body of the human consciousness.

He explained about the changes which have to be made in order to live with the shift that will occur in the body by going beyond the fourth dimension to fifth dimension. For that Babaji guided to choose oneness from time to time. You are going to live your truth as a Creator God. You are consciously participating in the creation of this existence.

Thank you Babaji!

1 MAGICAL ENCOUNTER WITH MAHAVATAR BABAJI

What words are enough to describe about Babaji. What can I say about Babaji. It was his grace that I was able to connect with him. Paying my due respect to Mahavatar Babaji, I shall describe my first meeting with Babaji. My relationship with Mahavatar Babaji is not just a matter of this birth, it dates back to many lives. In this birth, how my consciousness connected with him may feel like a magical story. I started my meditation practice for forty days. My meditation experiences were profound and felt an immense inner peace. On 13th September 2010, I got a brochure invitation for a conference at Pyramid Valley International and I felt a connection with pyramids.

I reached Pyramid Valley in Bangaluru with some of my friends in 2010. I was surprised to see the huge pyramid and had experience its energy. I met Brahmarishi Subhash Patriji who was the founder of

PSSM (Pyramid Spiritual Society Movement) and was spreading Pyramid Energy throughout the Earth.

I was always attracted by the pyramid. There was a picture of Mahavatar Babaji inside the pyramid, and seeing it, I stood unshakable, wondering who he was? The picture was attracting me so much; the vibrations of love were pouring out and vibrating in the valley. It was Mahavatar Babaji's grace, that I was blessed with such divine experiences. My soul was very keen to know about him. I kept seeing him for five to six times in a day during the workshops.

My soul was yearning to meet him. On one hand, the energy of the pyramid and on the other hand, the energy of Mahavatar Babaji. The attraction of both the energies had entered my life together.

The event of my attainment of Nirvana took place in Pyramid Valley while doing our Morning Group Meditation inside the Pyramid on 1st October. Patriji announced my Enlightment in front of thousands of meditators. I had many deep spiritual experiences there. He stated that he got a Pyramid Master for the awakening and spreading of Meditation in North India. I have had many experiences of ascension in Pyramid Valley.

Babaji is such a unique Divine Consciousness that it is impossible to describe him with words.

Next day, on 2nd October, as I was sharing my meditation experiences with a senior master and at the same time, her six year old grandson was playing nearby. He came to me and started chatting with me that,

"I am a Buddha",

I also said, *"Yes, I am also that, I am a Buddha".* He further said, *"I am doing meditation with Mahavtar Babaji."*

With a miraculous flow of energy, I also started saying, *"Yes, I am also doing mediation with Babaji."*

He came close to me, touched my third eye and agreed, *"Yes, you are with Babaji."*

He further said, *"My third eye is opened."*

I answered, *"Yes, my third eye is also opened."* That time I was unaware of the meaning of Third Eye. After talking to him, I wondered about my answers, *"Who is Mahavtar Babaji?".* The little master told me about Babaji a little bit and showed his picture. It was the same picture which was hanging there. That picture was none other than Mahavatar Babaji.

Next day I had vision of my life purpose and I came to know about my past life with Lord Buddha too. My Vision was clear, to teach and spread Meditation with Pyramid Energy.

☆☆☆

I came back to Delhi and started teaching meditation. Many times I remembered the incident with young boy. How spontaneously the same words came out of my mouth that, *"yes! I am also meditating with Babaji and I also live with Babaji"*. These words that came out of my mouth spontaneously were giving me some kind of information that I already have some relationship with him. The question that arose in my mind was how am I meditating with them and still meditating there. My physical body is here, then which body of mine is meditating with Babaji? Do I have any other body?

I was deeply reminded of Mahavatar Babaji. My mind was filled with feelings of love for Babaji and I wanted to see Babaji just once. I was very eager to meet Babaji. It seemed as if I was very anxious to meet him. My heart was completely immersed in Babaji's love. Strange kinds of emotions were coming in my mind in which there was pain, love and also yearning.

Some days later, I got a call from a friend of mine who lived in Calcutta and had come to Delhi for some work. He said, *"Asha, I'm coming to see you."* I said, *'Right away.'* He said, *'Yes, I am coming.'* It was 12 noon at that time and the place and time to meet him was fixed at 3–4 pm at Pizza Hut, Green Park Market.

When we met, I started telling him about all my feelings. While telling him about Babaji, I told him that, *"I have met Mahavatar Babaji. I'm yearning to meet him again. Don't know when Babaji will appear.*

In *which birth did I have a relationship with Babaji? My body meditates with Babaji and my body remains with Babaji only".*

Saying this, thinking, I asked him again, *"Is it possible that Babaji will give me darshan? can he hear me or can he see me? where is Babaji? will he meet me? I want to meet him, want to see him."*

Just then I felt as if two eyes were looking at me with great seriousness. This time I was just in my own bodily space. But those two eyes were looking at me. As soon as I looked at my friend in front of me, I saw that it was not my friend's eyes.

His eyes changed its position and colour of Emotions, they were Babaji's eyes and as soon as my eyes contact with Babaji's eyes, I was stunned. My eyes, wet with tears, were just staring at him like a Chakori bird looks at the moon.

On seeing Babaji, I felt as if I had found someone close to me. It felt as if someone who had been lost for a long time had come in front of me. My heart started blooming like flowers. It felt as if the Chatak bird got a drop of Swati Nakshatra and its thirst of many births was quenched.

I felt as if I was drowning in the pure love and unconditional ocean of Bliss. Tears were flowing drop by drop from my eyes, in front of everyone and they were not stopping. His presence was insuring me that Babaji is beyond this material world. He may be present at any time with his Glory.

I cried and said, *"Babaji, you? Babaji, you have come to meet with me."* I could not see anything around. The whole world was not present for me. Just myself and Babaji.

In this way my friend had also experienced this. He hugged me lovingly and said, *"It is an Encounter with Master, your consciousness witnessed that Immortal Babaji."* Then he shared his experience with me that he too had received Babaji message. Babaji himself had indicated to set up meeting at this place, which was only an hour away from my house. In this way Babaji appeared before me.

Now a new journey of my life has started under the guidance of Babaji. There was happiness on my face, a joyful moment forever. I now knew that the further path of my life would be under his direction. For me, going to Bangalore at Pyramid Valley, was the inauguration of my life's purpose. I was blessed. My life had become blessed. My birth was also blessed, that in this way Babaji, with whom I was related for many births, gave me his darshan. This was a matter of great fortune for me.

I had started my spiritual service for society by teaching Breath Meditation and constructing Pyramids. I was busy in the work of making my pyramids. But sometimes, I used to wonder whether the people of North India would be able to understand and be interested about knowing the pyramid energy. Many times, I used to have doubts about the mission of my life.

It is said that Guru is always with you, it was as if Mahavatar Baba Ji had chosen me and given me his divine guidance.

I remember one afternoon while meditating in our Bedroom. I saw Mahavatar Babaji along with five other Gurus entering my house and were walking very fast towards my room. All these Great Yogis sat together in a circle and meditated with us.

During meditation, my entire energy along with my house got transformed. I immediately felt uplifted, then I understood that Babaji's flowing energy will work for us throughout our life. At that time there was a question in my mind that who would listen about meditation because at that time no one was attracted towards meditation.

Then Babaji reassured me and I felt his energies entering through crown chakra into my whole body. Now I was able to see him, hear him and even feel him.

Babaji has guided me most of the time, and I have always followed his commands. I have had many experiences with Babaji over the years. I was completely speechless after hearing his voice, as if I suddenly touching the limitless sky. The light of the sun has brightened, showering us with the Golden lights of Ascension. Each time, it brings a new light and a new experience.

Thank you Babaji!

2 FREEDOM FROM FEAR

First of all Mahavatar Babaji talks about freedom. According to Babaji, the first freedom is victory over one's fear. This is a kind of bravery which is necessary for every work. A person remains afraid due to his ignorance because he does not understand that as long as a person is afraid, he cannot achieve his higher status. He is actually afraid because he is ignorant of his truth. That is why, he will have to free his consciousness from all fears and become fearless.

In 2011, the work of liberating or cleansing my mind and body from all the fear energies releasing. Although I was not afraid of anyone. I have had many unknown experiences with different types of energies. At midnight, I was asked to go visit random places. These types of experiences, which were happening to me at an uncertain place at an uncertain time, used to astonish me.

On October 10, 2011, we traveled from Coorg and reached Pyramid Valley. It was three o'clock in the night and it was raining heavily. Gupta ji and I were staying in the dormitory of Pyramid Valley. The entire dormitory was empty and no one was there.

I was trying to sleep in my room when suddenly I started seeing hundreds of eyes. Those eyes were saying something. Those eyes seemed to be those of Mahavatar Babaji, as if they were trying to tell me something. All I could see were eyes and eyes. Those eyes were indicating me to go to the penance place. It was three o'clock in the night. I got scared and tried to sleep again.

The next day, while meditating in the pyramid, I remembered Babaji, apologized and requested him to tell me what message he was giving me. Then Babaji gave me the word *"FREEDOM"*. He gave the message that not only you are scared but the entire human race is scared. Everybody is filled with fear. I again apologized to Babaji and said that from now onwards, I will not be afraid of anything. Wherever you will call me, I will come there.

Mahavatar Babaji took me to Tapasthali and showed me that the Pyramid Valley has become a portal. All the masters here are souls born with a part of the life force of Gods, Goddesses and Sages. I could see all the Gods, Goddesses and Sages. He said that a family of awakened souls is gathering to spread new life on the earth. His silent gesture indicated change.

Thus, this experience was a definite step on the ladder of my own development. My ignorance was the cause of my fear, that is why according to Babaji, a person needs double dose of bravery to face fear. At the same time, it is also a true study of the cosmology of its existence.

☆☆☆

There are many things present in the human body that depletes energy and make it weak. These are not only in his aura or body but also in his environment. The existence of all these parasitic creatures creates a feeling of unworthiness in the individual. For this reason, man starts considering himself unworthy at some subtle level.

Just as these parasites create patterns in the physical consciousness, similar patterns are seen in the consciousness of the brain which weakens a person's electromagnetic energy field. It can occur in any of the seven bodies of a person. Similarly, it also occurs in various body parts, in the main meridians of the body, in different energies, in the chakras and in the energy field of the nadis.

☆☆☆

Then there are many things to be worked on like impressions, memories, holograms, mental or emotional patterns and their programming. Similarly within the energetic aura, traces and memories of past lives, structures of the light body, cellular system, cellular bodies, DNA and genetic code, there is the apparent purpose of illness, negative self-talk and many more. These are special kinds of cleaning that require a very deep cleanse.

These are form of various parasites or energies of another human being or other types of energies that we are carrying with us in our body. In a way, it creates a patch on our body which sticks to different parts of our body. There are similar energies in different places of Mother Earth on which we have to work. In this way, work has to be done by meditating for a long time at different places and at different times.

Suppose if any disaster occurs somewhere, what kind of memory patch will be created at that place? If anywhere there is flood, earthquake etc., it will cause devastation there. This is how memory patches will be formed in the energies of that place.

Babaji explains this by saying that we are Multidimensional Beings. Addressing me he says, *"Asha, when I called you to the penance in the rain at night, you were scared but you have already attained Nirvana."* That means there was still some fear left within me.

Through this experience of 2011, he explained to me that this is the first spiritual experience a meditator has in the brain at the center of the forehead during deep meditation and that it is not limited to planet Earth. After attaining Nirvana, I had experienced that my consciousness is not only limited to this earth. Rather, I am the entire universe and at a higher position. Enlightenment is a form of elimination because it affects the present moment. That is why Babaji says to come out of your fears.

Babaji, while relating the fear of today's humanity, says that they have no knowledge of their own fear. They don't know how many fears they have. They are afraid of diseases. They are afraid of even death, because they are afraid of what will happen after death. They don't even know the cause of their diseases. If a person understands the events of his life well then, he becomes fearless from his fears! That's why you have to understand why you are afraid. If you are afraid of lightning, then this incident may be related to your previous life. Fear exists only within your cellular body, so remove it from within and clean it. Babaji was clearly talking about the DNA and its different layers.

☆☆☆

Babaji says more clearly that, now there is no need for any human being to be afraid of any other human being. If any individual or nation on the whole earth studies the true cosmic teachings of Krishna, Jesus, Buddha or any other Master, then that nation or individual will not only stand out but will be way ahead of other entities.

At the same time, that unit – individual or nation – will fearlessly maintain relationships with other nations all over the earth. If a nation becomes prepared like this, then that nation will have such national consciousness that it will be free from all its fears and will become fearless.

At the same time, that nation alone will be ready to show the path to the whole world, for this we all will have to understand and transform the energies sitting within us. If you imagine such a world, then get rid of all the fears within you.

Not only did all these experiences happen in Pyramid Valley, Babaji also appeared in the courtyard of my house along with Ganga. He also performed yagna at our house. Our house also became a portal. I shared all these experiences with Patri Ji also. He took a complete tour of our house, looked up and told us that our house has also become a portal. Now whatever messages I get, I will get them here only. I asked Sir, *"Is only my house a portal?"* Patri Sir replied with a smile, *"Wherever you stand, a portal will be created there. Wherever your feet touches, that is a portal."*

I used to listen to everything said by Patri Sir very carefully and I do so even today. According to him, this work is progressing at a very fast pace. Mahavatar Babaji reminds us that we are not low-vibrational beings. We must recognize and believe that we are quantum beings. If we are unwilling to think this way, we will not be able to open ourselves to higher consciousness.

Thank you Babaji!

3 PRESENT CONSCIOUSNESS AWAKENING

In my experiences with Mahavatar Babaji, Babaji told me many things. I am left speechless after hearing his voice. Like the light of the sun suddenly rises in the sky and every time it gives me a new light and a new experience. This time, in 2011, Babaji called me to his cave. Babaji said, *"You have to come and stay here."* I did not have any information about Babaji's cave.

I told my husband, Gupta Ji, about visiting Babaji Cave and my encounter with Babaji's energy, and he immediately agreed. We found out where this place was and then after that we went there for 10 days. We reached *"Kukuchina"* which is approximately fifty kilometers from Ranikhet. We just kept our luggage in the room and gone directly towards our destination where Babaji's invitation awaited us.

Now let's start the whole magical journey towards Babaji cave. Babaji's existence was magical as if you were going to the mountains and suddenly the wind changed. Every atom of the place was at peace and witnessing the presence of Babaji. His arrival happens in such a way that the entire clouds start rotating in a strange manner. It appears as if the sound of the winds has changed. Some of such scenes start to haunt us in a way that did not happen ever before. There was a strange sound in the air when he arrived. He was appearing in the air in the form of air and disappearing in the air.

My consciousness was slowly surrendering and losing. When he came, I recognized his voice very well. A strange kind of buzzing begins in the ears. The whole scenery was changing. Sunset light in the sky, shining with its beautiful colors. Yogananda Satsang Society place was near to us. We both sat down on one big rock and just witnessing the zero-point state.

No one was there. It was evening, and the cave's closing time was 5 PM. Again, we got up and continued to trek towards Babaji's cave. We were in front of Babaji's cave for the first time, we bowed down and with gratitude, we entered the cave and sat for meditation. There was total silence and I was going into trance. I saw Babaji in the cave, he was smiling and speaking about the cave. He took me to the inner part of the cave.

The cave was deep and beyond the cave, mountains were covered with snow. I started feeling so cold. I felt like I had been here many times before also. There are many very pure energy center and Babaji's cave is one of them. They immediately can bring an uplifting and elevation. After this magical experience, we felt uplifted, we both got up and came out. Our returning way was full of divine experience. I was able to see those invisible saints who were going towards the cave in the late evening. The time was about 6:30 p.m.

We used to go to Babaji's cave every day for the practice of meditation. One day, we also felt Lahiri Mahasaya Ji's energy around our place of stay.

While in the cave, Babaji gave me a one rupee coin. But, my physical intellect understood that Babaji was giving me wealth and money. The meaning of money is taught to us that money is Goddess Lakshmi. I was not able to understand the meaning of the coin shown by Babaji. But, no! Babaji was preparing us for the fifth dimension. Today, when I see all this, the experiences given by Babaji makes me realize how humans have to go through a period of change. This experience was just a hint of the fifth dimension.

We used to meditate every night during our stay near Babaji's caves. We felt Lahiri Mahashya energies there. A French couple was also staying where we were staying. The next day, I saw that he was making a mandala painting. I looked at his picture, it was absolutely round, just like my coin. I wanted to know from him about that art of painting and asked him to teach it. He said that this is an example of mandala art, but he cannot teach me this art because it is taught only to teachers, painters and service workers.

I stubbornly said that painting was my subject and prayed to Babaji in my mind. Then the couple showed me a design and asked me to tell what I feel after seeing this mandala.

There was a circular shape on that mandala all around and many buddhas were sitting around too. Seeing that, I replied that it seems as if many Buddhas are going to be born on earth. All the Buddhas are performing meditation and sacrifice on earth with collective consciousness. He immediately decided to teach me and in those ten days I learned the entire mandala painting art.

Here, Babaji wanted to tell through the rupee coin that like the rupee coin, the Mandala is also round. At the same time, Babaji also wanted to say that the human beings on earth need to balance themselves in this way. Through Mandala painting a person works to establish harmony between his left and right brain. Babaji was explaining that people all over the world are mentally distressed. They need mental balance, for which Mandala is very effective.

Mandala is a special type of sacred structure that has been used throughout thousands of years of known history on planet Earth and the entire universe because the entire creation is a Mandala. This Mandala structure acts as a pathway between the different dimensions of the earth and the universe and between the macro and micro worlds. This pulsating chakra is an eternal flow of cosmic energy that flows in and out of the chakra, just like an in-breath and an out-breath.

In this way, Mandala painting art reveals the path for a person to know thyself, truth, path of joy, ascension, purpose of life and for progress and development in physical and spiritual life. Our thoughts, words, actions and feelings come from your belief system about yourself and about the world. You are conscious being acting with awareness, but your subconscious mind is the creator.

When a person fully generated with wisdom, he will feed like a fire within, burning away all old patterns, their shadows from the deep past of other life times as well as this life time also, you may break or carry over from ancient times by Mandala Art. Almost all humans can clear their consciousness of old beliefs and attitudes.

After coming back from Babaji's cave, at Delhi, I started classes on Mandala art and getting Mandala art done along with meditation. After that, I experienced a lot of changes in my consciousness as well as in all the students. I realized that while doing Mandala art we practice living in the present moment. Because while doing Mandala art, we do not have to choose colours according to our logical mind. Rather, we have to fill the painting using whatever colour suddenly attracts us.

This means that whichever colour is lacking in our aura, we will choose that colour. Out of the seven colours in our aura, whichever colour is missing or does not exist, we will be attracted towards that colour. Here, Babaji was giving a hint to balance one's aura along with the conscious and subconscious mind.

Conscious mind and subconscious mind are two areas of activities of our mind. The conscious mind is called the logical mind, and the subconscious mind is called the illogical and creative mind. While remaining at the conscious level, the thoughts of the mind keep going to the subconscious level.

As soon as the subconscious mind receives our positive or negative thoughts, it starts acting on them and reacts accordingly. In this way the subconscious mind is the center of our emotions and works creatively. Our subconscious mind accepts only what is imprinted on it or what we consciously believe.

My clairaudience and clairlognizance divine ability were connecting my consciousness with Babaji. He was giving knowledge about the work of cleaning our mind by connecting conscious and subconscious mind with the present moment. He was telling us how we have to clear what is in our conscious mind and subconscious mind by living in the present moment.

During those ten days in 2011, when I went to meet Babaji in his cave and learned Mandala painting, I was experiencing something new every moment. Seeing the beds of roses, hearing the sound of whirlpools, at night, in the room, on my bed, everywhere, it seems as if Babaji is absolutely around me every moment. Sometimes I could feel fragrance around me, sometimes something else was being experienced. In such a situation, that moment has to be lived in now moment.

While living in that moment, we understand what impulse is coming within us, which fragrance is coming, what we are able to absorb at that particular moment. The time in 2011 when I saw Babaji's cave for the first time and after seeing it, I hummed a song with love that said *"Babaji, I will build a house in front of your cave, I will build a pyramid in front of your cave."*

Mahavatar Babaji gave me a message, *"Yes, I am always there in the cave. I already know that you all are coming. I call you. Do you think that I only live in caves? No, I am everywhere."*

On that day, I was seeing Babaji smiling in every flower, branch and in every particle of Dunagiri. I could feel him in the sky and in the clouds. I was feeling his presence everywhere. Sometimes I felt like he was right there with me, sometimes he was behind me and sometimes in front of me. He is there as it is. When I was closing my eyes, I was feeling that he is there in front of me and when I was opening my eyes I was feeling his presence.

I still remember when I told Babaji, *"I will build a house in front of your cave, and I will build a pyramid there. I want pyramids all over the world, as they will energize the entire Earth. I want pyramids everywhere."* Babaji smiled and asked, *"What will happen if the pyramids are built?"*

I replied, *"They will give power to whoever sits and meditates, and it will help them a lot."*

Then he asked, *"Then?"*

I said, *"They will have profound experiences during meditation."*

He asked again, *"Then?"*

I answered, *"They will become wise."*

Babaji asked once more, *"Then?"*

I replied, *"They will know themselves, they will know the truth."*

He asked again, *"And then?"*

I said, *"They will learn to live in the present moment. They will understand the power and importance of this moment. They will realize that they are simply present in the moment, and it is in that moment that they will meet themselves."*

Babaji then said, *"Now, look carefully at this place, the nature around you, and every particle where you feel my presence. I am right here. You are able to experience this because you are in the present moment, and that is why you can see me. Just like that, when any seeker, through meditation, reaches that state, they will be able to see me."*

Somewhere in those words, Babaji gave me a message, *"those who wish to meet him, see him, feel his presence, why are they unable to do so?"*

☆☆☆

Then after returning to Delhi after a month, a gentleman whose auspicious name was "Piyush", came to meet me at my house and took information from me about the pyramid. I gifted him a 2x2 golden pyramid and while giving it to him I said that I want a pyramid from you in Dronagiri, Kukuchina where Babaji's cave is located.

I came to know that a resort is being built in that area itself. Piyush Ji promised me that he will definitely do the work of building the pyramid. And today, the construction work of the pyramid in front of Babaji's cave is completed, which was named by Piyush ji as *"Asha Pyramid"*, I Hope of the whole world. Perhaps I feel myself that I am that hope who wants to fill everyone's heart with the color of miraculous thoughts filled with positivity because this color is gifted to me by Babaji.

In this way, this promise was fulfilled with Babaji's blessings at the very first meeting and the pyramid came up just opposite to the hills of Babaji's cave. Every year many Kriya Yogis from India and abroad come and stay and take advantage of the energy of the pyramid.

So, at that moment when the desire to build a pyramid awakened in my heart, my consciousness got connected to it and it was also fulfilled. In this way the energy completes its work.

Thank you Babaji!

4 CONNECTING BEYOND

In "Mahavatar Babaji Speaks" *book,* my dear readers, I am sharing, my experiences with Babaji. These experiences, as I mentioned, are connected to the fifth dimension and hold a deeper meaning. That meaning has always been present. Now, as I recount my experiences, I realize that a Jeevatma, takes birth many times, carrying its own soul connections. It is as if we are continuously linked to ourselves, our past lives, shaping our journey through the flow of energy.

My relationship with Babaji is an ancient one. This particular incident took place in 2011, on the day of Vasant Panchami. That day, I felt an inner pull, a strong calling from the Ganga, as if some divine power was summoning me to Rishikesh. I was deeply immersed in this feeling, as if I was being guided, yet I had no idea how to reach there or how the journey would unfold. During my meditation, I simply released a thought into the universe,

"If a higher power is calling me there, then I surrender to its will. Show me the path, and I will follow."

I believe that when we set such an intention, the universe listens. It absorbs our desire like an imprint on stone, aligning us with *"All that there is."* Not only do we connect with this vast cosmic energy, but also with Mother Earth and a higher state of consciousness. I had faith in this process, and my belief was soon validated. Within just two or three hours, I received an unexpected call from Bhubaneswar, where my younger sister lives. Her husband had just arrived in Delhi and was planning a trip to Haridwar. He asked, *"Would you like to join me? There's space in the car for five or six people."* He had already invited my other sister and my mother. And just like that, within hours, a journey to Haridwar unfolded, completely unplanned, yet perfectly orchestrated.

By evening, the four of us—my sister, my mother, my brother-in-law, and I, set off for Haridwar. Upon reaching, we checked into a hotel and rested for the night, as it was already late. Our journey had just begun. We stayed there for the night.

The next morning, as I woke up, I felt a sudden flow of energy in my mind, an overwhelming sense that my father was alive. Though he was no longer in physical form, his presence felt vivid. There was an ashram where he used to stay, and we all wanted to visit it. I had been there before, perhaps 12 to 15 years ago. Looking at the year 2011, I realized it must have been in 1997 when I last visited that place. Even though I hadn't meditated back then, I still felt a deep connection to it. I remembered it well.

At night, I used to sense the *Guru Shakti* of that place, an awakened energy. The ashram was ancient, nearly 300 to 400 years old. That was in 1997. Now, in 2011, the three of us set off for Rishikesh and made our way directly to the ashram. We searched for the ashram, as there was nothing particularly striking about it from the outside, but eventually, we found it. When we arrived, the Guruji was sitting there, overseeing the ashram's activities. I walked around, looking at the pictures on the walls in the puja room, where the asanas of past gurus were placed. The space was exactly as I remembered.

Then, we sat down to talk with Guruji. By this time, I had started my meditation practice, which began in 2010. I shared my experiences with him, the moments of deep meditation, my journey through Pyramid Valley, and the glimpses of enlightenment I had encountered.

As we spoke, I suddenly thought of *Mahavatar Babaji*. Guruji then said something profound, *"The tradition of Mahavatar Babaji and the gurus of this ashram are one and the same."* As he spoke about these ancient traditions, I felt a deep connection, like I was being reminded of something I had always known.

At one point, *Guruji* looked at me and gestured knowingly. "*Yes, he is the one*", he said. Then, he invited me to meditate in a special room. Inside, there were small idols of deities, pictures of revered gurus, a throne, and a simple bed. I entered the room and sat down to meditate, while my mother and sister remained outside. The moment I closed my eyes, a vision unfolded. I saw two radiant beings standing before me. They were dressed in traditional dhotis, with long flowing hair. They reached out and touched both of my hands. In the next instant, we were flying through the sky. We had left the ashram, rising above the earth, moving effortlessly through the vast expanse. The stars, the moon, the sun, all passed by as we travelled beyond the limits of time and space. Through the clouds, we soared higher. After a while, we landed in an unfamiliar place. In front of me stood a cave, its entrance dark and mysterious.

During the time when I was flying, I had felt an intense shivering sensation, a deep coldness enveloping my body. Now, standing at the mouth of the cave, I still carried that strange energy within me. Without hesitation, we stepped inside. As we moved deeper into the cave, I saw a guru sitting before me. He was dressed in white, though I couldn't recall whether he wore a full robe or just a dhoti with his upper body bare. He looked at me and smiled warmly. He said, *"You came, my child."* He gestured for me to sit beside him, and as I did, I felt an overwhelming sense of peace. It was as if he was pleased with me.

I glanced around the cave, taking in my surroundings. Though I could not remember much, one thing stood out, a shining silver statue. I examined it closely. It was a statue of a Devi, a divine feminine presence, but I couldn't recognize which deity it was. The statue radiated an ethereal glow, its silvery-white brilliance captivating me.

After spending some time in this sacred space, I felt myself returning back through the sky. My meditation ended, and as I opened my eyes, I looked around the room to see if there was anything white or silver like the statue I had just seen. But there was nothing.

I stepped out of the meditation room and approached Swamiji, who had been sitting outside. Excitedly, I began recounting my experience, the entire vision I had witnessed in just 15 or 20 minutes.

As we sat there, I suddenly noticed a young man stepping out of a nearby room. He had a broad chest, long hair, and looked to be around 22 or 23 years old. He walked out briskly and disappeared beyond the ashram. The moment I saw him, an intense realization struck me. Overcome with emotion, I shouted, *"Babaji! Mahavatar Babaji! It was him,*

I have seen Babaji!" I turned to Swamiji and asked, *"Tell me, who stays in that room?"*

We had been sitting there for an hour, and except for Swamiji, the ashram had been completely empty. No one else was there. But Swamiji shook his head. *"There is no one here"*, he said.

"No, that's not possible," I insisted. "I just saw him come out of that room and walk away so quickly. Who else could it be?" Yet, he kept repeating, *"There is no one here."*

A chill spread across my forehead. My heart pounded. Tears of joy welled up in my eyes. I closed my eyes again, and everything became clear. I had been taken to Babaji's cave, and to confirm this divine experience, Mahavatar Babaji himself had appeared before me. It was a seal of truth, proof that what I had seen was real.

☆☆☆

Even now, as I write these words, my body feels the same sensations I experienced that day. My breath is deep and steady, as if time has frozen, as if those sacred moments are unfolding before me once again. I long to relive that time, again and again. With this experience engraved in my soul, I made my way back to Haridwar.

As we returned from Haridwar, still immersed in the profound experience of the day, evening approached. It was around 5 o'clock when we decided to visit the Ganga Ghat. The three of us sat down on the steps near the river, watching the waves of Mother Ganga gently flow. The beauty of the sacred river filled me with an overwhelming sense of peace. I gazed at Mother Ganga, lost in the serenity of the moment.

Suddenly, the rhythmic beat of a loud drum echoed from behind, as if announcing the arrival of a majestic presence. I turned around, curious to see what was happening. Someone whispered, *"Ganga Ji's ride is coming."* As I laid eyes on the ride, a shiver ran through me, it was as if the vision I had experienced that morning was manifesting before me.

In my meditation, I had been taken to Babaji's cave, where I had seen a shining silver idol of a Devi and the same idol was coming in that ride, Mother Ganga. And now, here she was, Mother Ganga's divine presence being honored. As the ride passed, the grand aarti began. On the edge of the Ghat, the pandits held massive lamps, lighting them in unison as they performed the Ganga Aarti.

I was overwhelmed, and I said, *"Today, I want to perform Mother Ganga's aarti with a overwhelming heart."* I took one of the large lamps and held it in my hands. As I moved the flame in reverence, my gaze shifted, sometimes to the sky, sometimes to the earth, and sometimes to the flowing waters of Ganga. Tears welled up in my eyes. This experience was given to me by Mahavatar Babaji.

He had guided me beyond the physical realm, allowing me to witness his sacred place through astral body travel, he had revealed himself to me in his physical form and helped me recognize the divinity of Mother Ganga. At that moment, everything became clear. The cave, the idol, the presence, each piece fell into place.

So now, you all can finally understand who Babaji is, the energy behind him, how he recognizes his children and devotees and show his grace on them.

A deep transformation took place within me. It felt as if every cell of my body, every strand of my DNA, had been awakened. Something long hidden within me had come alive. It was as if I had been initiated and attuned to the vast creative power within me. I felt as if, my awakened DNA, has brought so many high vibrations, inside me. I feel, this is a process of manifestation, creation, and it is becoming so instant. And I, even if I am not aware of the consequences of this creation, then there can be such situations, where we, by using that information, which becomes the reason, we can reach the heights of our consciousness.

If I had not been aware of the consciousness and inner voice calling me to Haridwar while in Delhi, or if my physical body was not ready, or if I had not agreed with an open mind, then this experience might never have happened.

I feel as if I was ready to work with the layers of my DNA. I truly hold tremendous creative power within me. It amazes me to think about what a single thought can create when my DNA strands are activated and ready to receive. It was hidden and secret, yet it revealed itself to my consciousness, allowing me to acknowledge this experience.

Thank you Babaji!

5 HIGHER POTENTIALS WITHIN

It was in year 2012, we had come to Bengaluru Pyramid Valley for the Global Conference of Spiritual Scientists. The entire program has ended and very few people were left in the Pyramid Valley. There were hardly 8-10 people left, everyone had gone and there was an atmosphere of complete peace in the entire Pyramid Valley.

The next day there was a workshop in Pyramid Valley which explained about Aura. A master had come from abroad to talk on this topic. As soon as that class about body and aura science got over, I felt like going to the place of Tapasthali. It is a place at a high altitude which can be reached after trekking for about an hour. There is a statue of Lord Shiva. I asked my husband Gupta Ji and my daughter Devika for trekking. The other four Pyramid Masters also joined us. When we reached Tapastali, we started meditating on the rocks. While meditating there,

I felt as if some mantras were being chanted under these rocks. I felt those voices under the rocks.

I was feeling such an energy at that place as if many yogis were sitting there and doing yoga-tapasya. One person among us also started channeling Babaji and he started giving Babaji's message in a strange voice, which was in a completely different kind of voice.

As soon as the channeling process was over, we all got up and started looking towards the statue of Lord Shiva. Then from a distance in the sky we felt that something was coming towards us and getting closer. It was nothing but a UFO - a flying saucer. Gupta Ji called out loudly towards it, *"Come, come, we are ready, come to us. Come."* As if they were listening to us and looking at us.

They started coming towards us at very fast speed. Seeing Gupta Ji's transformation and his message, a different kind of energy came into my body. I felt complete tightness in my legs and the nerves in my knees tightened all of a sudden, as if I was waiting to see a very different kind of experience. And I was not even able to get ready for it.

Suddenly, fireworks were released in the sky like Diwali crackers. It was a wonderful sight, even though Diwali was not there, but the sky was celebrating Diwali, so far away from the city, something was happening suddenly at night when there was no festival, it was an absolutely wonderful sight. This sight continued for a long time. I had taken a Seven Up bottle to drink. As soon as I started opening the bottle, it suddenly shot upwards at great height, as if it was also celebrating. Nature was trying to show something in the presence of Mahavatar Babaji. On one side the messages of Mahavatar Babaji and the presence of Lord Shiva and on the other side the earth and sky were uniting. Also, the vibrations of the chanting of the ascetics were being felt inside the earth.

It seemed as if a moment had come when the core of the earth and the sky had become one and we were seeing this scene and happiness was being celebrated. It seemed as if the world was ending in 2012 according to the Mayan calendar and the Earth and all of us were entering into a new world and we were being welcomed. A celebration was being held on earth and we were being its witness.

Many people thought that 2012 was the end of the world, but the reality was that it was the beginning of a new awakening. It was October 2012, I didn't know about the Mayan calendar at that time. The supernatural awakening that I had at that time was actually part of a larger conscious light that was moving into the fifth dimensional matrix. We all have the ability to tap into the knowledge of our own great powers far out in the matrix of space.

There are many guides available to us to serve us as we map this world and take ourselves into the fifth dimension. I think more people than ever before are getting ready for their ascent.

The UFO sightings were meant to make us realise that not only do we live in a multi-dimensional world but we can communicate with other planets. We can also communicate with God.

We choose whether we want to move forward or not. We have to raise our consciousness forward. As we continue this, our abilities to reach higher dimensions and higher states of consciousness increase and thus we can define ourselves, our consciousness, and our DNA at a much faster rate than ever before.

We choose the dimension in which we are at any given time and the state of our mind at that time. At that time, we were very close to our ascension and the experience given by Babaji had given us a kind of ascension. In this way, we realised that there were some of us who have already ascended in which they will manifest their supernatural powers in positive ways. But it is true that we are all shifting into a new energetic space. We are shifting towards a consciousness where there is love and joy.

All seven of us who were with me had experienced this. We are spiritually in what we call the third dimension where there is all kind of artificial intelligence, technologies, where there is pain, where there is duality, there is disease, there is anger, there is greed and together there is the mind, by which we are controlled. But there is no spirituality in the third dimension. The world that was shown to us and connected to us through UFOs, took us into a dimension where possibility was shown. The possibility was shown that time has come to prepare yourself for it. There were fireworks in the sky and the seven up went so high that meant we won. Now we've come out of a time that had to end and there's a celebration like this.

We were descending and this question was coming to our mind: why didn't they descend near us? Why didn't they come towards us? Gupta Ji was calling them but I was not ready, I had set the intention for the UFO to just come close and go back after giving the experience. Due to my inner feeling, they did not come down to earth in front of us.

When we came down to the valley, we met two spiritual scientists in the cafeteria who were from America, Don Paris and Eric Bergland. We shared with them our experience because they were aware of the experiences of Americans about the changes that occur in the body after seeing a UFO. Don checked our pulses and our heartbeats and gave positive confirmation of UFO contact. He knew this science. So, this experience given by Babaji gave us the message of the shift into the fifth dimension. When truth layer is activated, you live your truth. You consciously participate in the creation of this universe. We have to believe that we are grand beings with many higher potentials and possibilities too.

Thank you Babaji!

6 CLEANSING YOUR AURIC FIELD

In 2013, Mahavatar Babaji's work is for public welfare. He communicates with the consciousnesses with whom he meets, through signs, through visuals or through his words. Babaji can appear anywhere. It is not at all true that Babaji is at one place only. I have felt Babaji's energy many times at my home and have also seen him. Although for the first time he invited me to his cave. We stayed there for 10 days and also experienced Mandala art. Every two years Babaji calls me to his cave.

Once a tour was planned from Dehradun with Patri sir for Babaji's cave. Sir was always busy in some program or the other. I proposed to him to accompany me to Babaji's cave. But Patri Sir refused due to the reason that there is a lot of height and climbing. Patri Sir read my mind. Then after two minutes Sir said yes for the tour and said, *"Okay, we will go."* It was a journey for 9–10 days. Various meditation programs were arranged by Guptaji in Haridwar, Kosani and Haldwani too. Patriji was very happy after his first Ganga Arti at Parmarth Niketan.

Early in the morning we started our yatra from our hotel in Haldwani towards Babaji's cave. I experienced the bursting energies of spring. Sun was rising with its golden rays and mother earth was so happy to feel the warm touch. Our car was running up above the hills and snow covered mountains started appearing in front of us. We all were so overwhelmed.

A very beautiful experience was given by Babaji while walking with Patri Sir in 2013. Nanda Ji had also come with a group from South India and all of us from North India had gathered at Babaji's place. As soon as we started climbing, Patri Sir led everyone forward. They were sending everyone forward. I arrived a little late. I saw Patri Ji sitting on a rock waiting for us. As soon as Patri Ji saw me, Devika and Gupta Ji, he called and asked us to sit. Patri sir wished to drink something. I had a bottle of Fanta, a soft drink. I gave it to Sir. Sir drank it and as Sir was drinking it, a voice was coming in my ears, *"I am coming"*, it seemed as if Babaji was speaking, *"I am coming, today I will take you myself along with me to my cave."*

I was wondering, who is with me at this time? On one hand, Patri Sir has sent everyone ahead and on the other a voice is coming in my ears, *"I am coming."* I started looking around. Babaji will come, but in what form will Babaji come? Then my attention went towards Patri Ji. His physical body instantly changed. Mahavatar Babaji had come within our beloved Guruvar, Pitamah Patri Ji.

Patri Sir's entire body changed completely. A minute ago, he was walking and standing straight, but now his entire waist was completely bent. He had become an old man and could not even walk. Patri Sir had become as if he was a four or five hundred year old man. Patri sir was also talking in a completely different way. I had never seen Patri Sir blessing anyone. But, while blessing us, he placed his hand on our heads and gave so many good wishes to fulfill our life purpose.

Patri Sir used to walk four steps and then he would sit down because his energies were Mahavatar Babaji's energies. He walked slowly all the way and as soon as he saw Yogananda Ashram, Patri Ji laid down to rest.

That day Babaji gave many messages in his cave. Babaji gave a message for Cleansing, that due to changes in nature on earth, cutting of trees and plants, as well as pollution of rivers and human nature, there is a need for cleansing them.

That same day I meditated three times in Babaji's cave. First, we climbed up and went to Babaji's place.

I meditated for the first time. The second time, when Patri Ji slowly climbed up, I meditated with him. When Patri Ji came down, Babaji called me again to his cave, then I meditated for the third time.

Whatever message Babaji gives us, I was receiving in the form of mental language and signs. Just as we connect mentally with each other through telepathy, we receive messages from Babaji in this way. Our vibration changes in a different way. Within us, we start seeing or hearing something in a different way and then we start accepting it. Suddenly the intensity of our vibrations starts changing.

Babaji gave the message for cleaning around the cave, then as soon as I came out of the cave, I took the pallu of my saree with my hands and started the cleaning work by wiping the trees and plants there. I experienced the same thing in meditation with Patri Sir also. Patri Ji also asked all the masters to clean the surrounding areas. Together we all cleaned there for about an hour.

I understood that there was uniformity in the message of cleanliness that both Babaji and Patriji were giving. Cleansing by our own effort, simply started showing me in other ways as knowing. We have our DNA, it depends how many layers are activating with knowing. Babaji was clearly talking about raising the consciousness. We know that double helix DNA found in every cell of our bodies which contains the blueprints for our physical bodies.

We have an additional ten strands of non-physical DNA to record the information. As we grow, they record the changes. We carry this information forward into our future lives. So, Babaji was showing us that cleanse your old layers of old belief patterns which are not serving you. Old fear based on paradigms can be replaced through expanded spiritual awareness. Belief is the key to your life that you create. If you believe that life is all positive, you will create positivity. There is so much carryover from your ancient times, you must break these old patterns.

Through this I want to say that if Mahavatar Babaji wants to come in front of you then he can condense himself in any form. In his light body he can appear anywhere and at any time. He can appear through the eyes of any person. That is why we have to awaken our consciousness so much through meditation that we can catch it, through any medium – smell, sound, perception or consciousness. The main thing is to accept their knowledge. So, are you ready to receive their knowledge?

Thank you Babaji!

7 MANIFESTATION FOR MOTHER EARTH

It was 2013, Babaji gave the message of plantation. His message was that many trees, along with a variety of fruits and flowering trees should be planted in the mountainous area around his cave.

I asked to Babaji, *"Babaji, everyone comes there for trekking. What will the fruit trees do there?"*

Babaji said, *"The time is coming when this place will become a pilgrimage site where many people will come to visit. Right now, many people do not know about this cave and this place. That is why you will have to plant fruit trees here."*

So, I accepted this by saying, *"Yes, Babaji."*

I went to the office of Yogoda Satsanga Committee in Dwarahat and informed them that Babaji had given a message that many fruits trees should be planted there.

On the other hand, the pyramid built by Piyush Ji was about to be completed. In the evening, he used to organise classes for children there, in which they run a Kindergarten for the children. I shared this experience with Piyush Ji. He says with a very beautiful thought, "Babaji's message to plant trees must be carried out. It will lead to prosperity." Then he told me in a very simple way that *"sister, we can give trees of orange, pomegranate, malta, etc. to the children there and also with the idea that as you are growing up, you will also plant these trees in the courtyard of your house. As you grow, these trees will also grow with you, so water them daily."*

I shared this experience with some meditators and I asked them to plant some fruits and flower trees for their next trip to Babaji's Cave. Then I got messages from many people that they have already planted rose flowers and many other trees there.

On one side, I could see trees towards Babaji's cave and on the other side, I was feeling that this knowledge is now spiritually ready for manifestation along with the meditation. Let's do it. Man can imagine a beautiful creation by calming his mind through his thoughts.

Through this experience, Babaji gave me the message that you have to sow new seeds. On one hand I had started creating crystal pyramids and on the other hand I was also propagating knowledge. Different meditation centers were also opened. By 2013, I had gone to different places with Patri Ji.

Here the meaning of new seeds was that people have to be connected with meditation and knowledge. Aham Brahmasmi means the state of sowing seeds.

As soon as I received this message, my work started more rapidly. DNA is information and it is time for people to accept that they are twelve-strand beings. When you work with your awakened self and understand yourself. Now you start understanding things fully and after this is connecting with the *"I AM"*, means connecting with the divine soul.

Babaji has said that we have to cleanse them all and connect them with sacred energies. Also, for all the earth-bound souls, spirits, energies that are in our body or in the body of Mother Earth, Babaji has directed all of us to do this process. For this we will have to do the work by connecting with Mother Earth. We have to connect with the energies and heartbeats of Mother Earth by feeling one with our own heartbeats and energies and then we have to heal ourselves and Mother Earth.Then finally those energies have to be sent from the earth in the direction where they need to go. Mahavtar Babaji was speaking about various cleansing processes for individuals and for the Earth also. Awakening together is the message.

Thank you Babaji!

8 NEW MISSION – SOUL PURPOSE

It was the year 2014, one day my husband Gupta Ji and my daughter Devika, all three of us were doing chain meditation together. After some time, while doing chain meditation, we started feeling as if all three of us were encountering energies of Brahma, Vishnu, Mahesh and then Mahavatar Babaji was in front of us. A yagna was performed in our house in the presence of Mahavatar Babaji.

There is an open courtyard in the middle of our house. In this open space first Mother Ganga purified us in a subtle form through the sky. The stream of Mother Ganga washed Gupta Ji completely. After that, they made Guptaji sit in the middle of the house and a very surprising process took place. All the yagya material was coming from the sky. It included Yagya Samidhas, Havan material, Kusha, puja materials, etc. A Yagya was performed in the presence of Mahavatar Babaji. After the Yagya was completed with complete rituals, a wonderful kind of energy change took place in our entire house. Along with the atmosphere of the house, all the vibrations of the three of us had also changed. When we narrated this experience to Patri Ji, he said that your entire place has been sanctified and a portal has been established at this place. Mahavatar Babaji's initiations were received in this way.

Cosmic energies contain very higher vibrations and when we integrate higher vibrations through our inner matrixes with the help of Babaji and Guides then naturally your consciousness is raised. In Breath Meditation, we receive cosmic energies from our own crown chakra into our bodies. Cosmic consciousness is available for us and it is being downloaded. Babaji helps and guides all the great souls who have taken birth in this world for public welfare work from time to time.

IN 2014, I got involved in the work of constructing the pyramids and teaching meditation across various parts of India, which was the purpose of my life in coming to Earth in this lifetime. In 2014, the work of my book *"NAVYUG MEI PYRAMID ENERGY"* completed and the book was released on March 10, 2014 at the Giza Pyramids in Egypt by Brahmarishi Patriji in Hindi language. This book was to be released in Egypt.

After two months, I went through a near death experience. That day, I came and sat in my drawing room in the evening. As soon as I sat on the sofa, I felt that suddenly two masters came and sat near me. I raised my face and started looking at those two masters. On one side of me was Mahavatar Babaji and on the other side was Jesus. Mahavatar Babaji gestured to me and said, *"Come, put your head on my shoulder."* So I placed my head on his shoulder. Babaji said, *"My child, your work is complete."* I answered positively. As soon as I put my head down, I felt lightness in my body and witnessed that my astral body was coming out of my physical body and I am going out of my drawing room with both of them and we are going through the sky. As soon as we were floating near the moon and stars, two more masters arrived. I saw Lord Shri Krishna and Patri ji. Patri ji said, *"This is my child. I will also take her with me."*

I was literally floating in the sky. On either side of me were Mahavatar Babaji and Jesus and behind me were Shri Krishna and Patri Ji. All the four masters took me to the place from which there is no return, the place when we merge into our source. This was the final state of our bodies and from where we never return. These are the very last moments. I was going there, and I reached. Suddenly, as I was entering that river of light, Babaji asked me, *"Do you have any desire?"* My astral body turned around and looked back.

That scene is still so vivid in front of my eyes as I looked back from that place, I could see my husband Gupta Ji on earth. One of his sentences was audible to my ears, *"Asha, I will not be able to live without you. We will go together."*

I was looking at him. I never used to agree with him and always answered that this was ignorance. Some shift took place in my consciousness. So as soon as I saw him, I immediately said to Babaji, *"Babaji, I have to work with nature and children on earth."* Now after one of my wishes has been fulfilled, I had set another mission in which I would love to work for nature and animals. I love animals very much and I wish that there are only animals in the whole forest and I could play with them. Whether it is a giraffe or a lion, whether it is an elephant, I enjoy playing with them.

As soon as I said that I wanted to work with children, Babaji said, *"Now I shall give you this blessing that I will come to take you only when you want."* By saying this I felt as if he left me and as soon as he left me, I entered into my physical body again in my drawing room. My neck which had become crooked was not getting straight and now it was slowly getting straight. It was a very amazing experience. Now I was going back to my room again. I checked the time on the clock.

About four hours had passed in this entire sequence of events. I was alone at home at that time. There was no one else at my house. My husband Gupta ji and Devika were not at home. About 4 hours had passed since they left.

So Mahavatar Babaji had given me this one blessing and a new mission in 2014.

I came back into life, came here again from that unbroken light. Babaji's message here was very special. Babaji asked and Babaji did it. Babaji asked my wish and Babaji gave me his blessings. Babaji says that man still considers himself a body and considers himself about to die. Man still believes in himself that if I have come into this world, I will fall ill, grow old and die. Death was not my wish, death for me is such a thing that whenever I will be called, I will go and I was called too. And now the same earth and the whole world have reached a state in which Babaji wanted us to give an opportunity to serve more, but there was not even the slightest fear in it and only information.

Whatever situation we are in, we have to look at it through meditation. Because till now in this dual world we see life and death. Life and death mean dying-living, coming-going. But our divinity which is coming out now, what is that divinity by which we can live as long as we want. We have divinity, we are ready to live as a divine soul. Will the decision taken by us affect only me or my consciousness or will it affect other consciousnesses as well? Dimensions are increasing at a very fast pace.

Maybe this is still a confusion for you guys. It is may be up to you whether you still believe in it or not. It may be that this world of duality is within the duality because the time we are in now is one step inside the fifth dimension & another one step inside the duality and in such a situation, we are pulling out of this timeline.

☆☆☆

This is how we have become so powerful. We do not believe that we are powerful. When Babaji asked me, *"Do you have a wish"*, then here my free will has come, then here has come the purpose of our life, then it has come whether we want to end the purpose of our lives. If life has no purpose, then life also ends.

But if we stretch the purpose of life and make it bigger, we add more links either in our free will or in the outline of our life or according to our will power or according to any power. We can come out from any position. Then such a great change happens inside us as it happened with me, I was released, that is, I was told that this is the opportunity for the rapid changes on earth. Don't let this slip away.

Recognize your divinity. You can come back whenever you want. That meant free will to die, free will to arrive and free will to leave the body. Here all those dualistic aspects which were sick, powerless, confused, lonely and disappointed are all left behind. Here I did not ask to go back out of attachment for love, but it was my choice that I wanted to work for nature and for the children of the world.

There were layers within layers here. Babaji had inaugurated all this. Babaji asked clearly whether you are ready. As soon as I listened to Babaji's message, there was a change in my consciousness within myself, but when you all are reading the pages of this book and seeing these words, then it is definitely your divinity.

That change is happening in me too. This is the change which is essential for this era. We do not get this divine transformation by looking at others but it comes from within. While our Gurus, our Masters remain in touch around us but the energy of our divinity, the awareness of our Supreme Soul, love is all in our hands. All of them have now become very close to us. But we are not paying attention. Leaving aside whatever is happening around us, whatever is being experienced, we start looking towards something where we wait to see. We look to the side waiting for something to come from. We see it, read it, understand it; But we have to decide this ourselves. What we need to know for ourselves is to feel our energy and our life starts happening according to the decisions we make at every moment.

According to that, great souls, divine souls, Mahavatar Babaji are only watching us. They are testing us. A Supreme Guru, a Mahavatar Babaji saw this and showed it by example. Now, if we do not accept the divine awareness within us, then it will also say that you have not played your game completely and then after a few days you will be lost in this world again. But again and again we should be ready to bring out our divinity. So, despite being with Gurus and Masters and having experiences with them, despite being in contact with them, despite listening to Babaji's words, even in their presence, we are still in that moment of our life, given by the Masters, moving forward into our divinity.

This is the divinity that Babaji has always talked about. Divinity is the right of every human being. Divinity is that part of us, within us and that is who we are. We should spend every moment living this. Remembering this, every moment will change our thoughts. Our mental body will change. All our reasons will end. All our actions will change. We will come to a royal path and start walking on such a path that no one would have experienced the joy derived from it till date. When we make our determination, the entire universe becomes ready to support us with our purpose. It happens.

What do you think my dear readers? What had happened to me? I returned after having my near-death experience. I created a new blueprint for myself. When I changed my blueprint, my vibrations raised.

Mahavatar Babaji gave me this experience to let the whole world know that we may intent and may change our blueprints.

I now recall Babaji's words from 2014 when he told me, *"Come whenever you feel ready."* At the time, I didn't fully grasp the depth of his message. He was speaking of regeneration, the ability to consciously communicate with our bodies, remove the imprint of death, and embrace our eternal nature. Just as we prepare and consume food with awareness, we can learn to communicate with our cells, guiding them toward renewal rather than decay.

This is the essence of the message Babaji entrusted to me, the realization that even while living on Earth, one can transcend the cycle of death and rebirth. The Earth itself is shifting into higher vibrations, and for the first time, this transformation is occurring without the usual process of separation. Babaji and Gurudev gave this message with unwavering faith, *"Remove the imprint of death from your being."*

This is the secret of regeneration. When Babaji let go of my hand in 2014 and sent me back to Earth, he entrusted me with a mission, to work with nature and guide others, especially children, toward this realization. He spoke of immortality, of our existence as multidimensional beings who have the power to choose their transition.

Death is not an end; it is merely a shift in consciousness. If we are truly divine souls, here with a purpose, then why do we forget our true nature? Babaji's teachings remind us, the way we pass from this world shapes our next existence. If we embrace death in fear, that fear carries over. But if we cultivate awareness, we can transcend it.

His final message was clear, *"You are immortal. You are multidimensional. You can choose your own departure from this realm, consciously and fearlessly."*

Thank you Babaji!

9 OPENING THE GRAND EYE WITH BALANCE

In the year 2017, on the day of Bhado Amavasya, there was worship of ancestors to be done in our house. After completing the puja work, since I got tired I went to my drawing room and lay down on my sofa to rest. I love relaxing on my couch. So as soon as I lied down, suddenly Babaji appeared in front of me. Babaji said, *"The time has come."*

I asked Babaji, *"what time has come?"*

Again he said, *"The time has come for people to know."*

I asked the question, *"What people should know Babaji"*.

Babaji said, *"the time has come for the people to know about me, to know about Mahavatar Babaji. People don't know anything yet. Ordinary people do not know about body, mind, soul, kriya yoga and about their condition. You have to tell everyone about me and introduce everyone to me."* I said,

"Yes Babaji. Everyone needs to be introduced to you." Babaji said, "A movie related to my life has to be made."

"Now energy of Love, Peace and Harmony are spreading on planet Earth. People who are here for service will start connecting with you. My children will start joining you and you start this service for humanity." After getting this message, I started creating small videos on my own.

After a month, Babaji again invited me to his cave with everyone and gave me a message regarding this. He said that you have to make a travel plan and bring who all are searching for me, in my cave. I said, *"Babaji, I will not be able to come this time. Just like you are telling me, please inform all those who want to come to you Babaji, because you can do everything."*

Babaji disagreed and said, *"No, you have to make efforts."* How and what to do. Thinking about all this, I talked to my husband. But when I asked him for this visit, he clearly refused. We cannot hide anything from our Guru. They know everything about us. Babaji treated me the way parents treat their children.

One night, when I was sleeping on my bed and I changed to my left side, he brought me down from the bed. Again, Babaji appeared in front of me and told me the same thing. Then I said, "Babaji, how can we bring anyone like this?" He said, *"No, you have to bring everyone."* Finally, I agreed with Babaji. *"But how will I do all this work?"* I asked Babaji. Then Babaji told to post the message on Facebook.

With Babaji's permission, I created an invitation poster to Babaji Cave and posted it on Facebook. I told my husband about the situation and we have decided to go to Babaji's cave. Gupta Ji asked me, *"Who would come?"* I said to him that I don't know who will come, but Babaji has said he knows who will come. It has to be done. After I posted the brochure on Facebook, more than 40 people came up from different places in India. Mumbai, Pune, Kolkata, Delhi, Punjab and all across the country. When those meditators and seekers were coming, Babaji had already notified me that, these are the people who will make further journeys with you to my place.

That means we must spread Babaji's message and then people will join the groups. We can see a tremendous increase in the number of people who started going to Babaji's caves after 2017. After that, spiritual trekking, journeys, talks, discussions and fairs started being organised there.

Later, everyone did this work as per Babaji's advice. Babaji told me that people do not know how to reach the caves and from where to start the journey and by which train, where to reach and start. For that, I will have to tell them about all that the roads that were open and how to reach Babaji's caves.

In this way, in 2017, Babaji gave the message for this campaign to further spread and propagate about Mahavatar Babaji and thus this work was done successfully. This was the month of October and we had to reach Rishikesh on 2nd November where we had a program.

As per the program, we all were going together to Babaji Cave but as soon as we reached the Delhi station, I suddenly saw a scene in the train that appeared in a pyramid shaped triangular layout. Babaji clearly said that you should not come directly from the station to caves. You have to come through this place where there is the temple of Lord Shiva. I was watching all this while sitting in the train. The train was about to reach Haldwani at 5:00 am.

When I got down at the station, more than five Innova vehicles accompanied us. At that moment, I did not know where we had to go. After getting down I asked some people about the temple of Lord Shiva in that area. I didn't even know the name of the temple. But few people there told me that there is Jageshwar Dham which is a very great pilgrimage place of Lord Shiva, 50 kilometers away from Almora.

The pyramid shaped route was from Kathgodam to Haidakhan Ashram, then to Jageshwar Dham, followed by Dunagiri Babaji Cave, and finally back to Delhi. I told everyone that I have to follow Babaji's guidance and go accordingly.

Four soul sisters joined me. Now Babaji's energies was with me while traveling in the car. We started the journey towards Jageshwar Dham.

As soon as we got down from the station, the path that was being shown to me, the place was Devalaya, a very great pilgrimage place of Lord Shiva.

The first place we reached on this journey was the Ashram of HaidaKhan Babaji, who is a form of Mahavatar Babaji.

Haidakhan is a small village which is located 33 kilometers away from Haldwani in the Kumaon region of the Himalayas. If we look at this place, then according to the Skanda Purana, Lord Shiva had a conversation with his son Kartikeya in this area and at this place. Lord Shiva arrived with Parvati where he stayed for a night.

This place is famously known as Kumaon Kailash, where the river Gautama Ganga flows. It is said that this river was brought here by Lord Shiva because this was previously underground. This Gautama Ganga River appeared in Haidakhan village which later came in contact with Sati Kund.

After we reached the ashram, I could experience a very different kind of feeling. I could see a cave in the ashram. There were different places in the ashram where Adi Shankaracharya Ji and many saints had come. Many yagyas were performed and many Yogiraj's had come there and the place had a different belief.

There was a place on the other side of the Gautam Ganga river, with a cave built on it. This cave's specialty was that there were many underground tunnels there which were connected to different places like Haridwar, Varanasi, Kailash Mansarovar. This is also mentioned in Shiva Purana and this cave is also used by Lord Shankar for intense penance.

I reached this cave and as soon as I stepped inside the cave, I saw Lord Shiva. It was a heart warming experience as if he hugged me and was saying, *"My bacha (child) is here!"* It was a very divine experience. I felt complete presence of Lord Shiva Energy with its full compassion and emotion towards me.

I totally surrendered myself to shiva's consciousness, only shiva and myself, merging at zero state. I was trying to get up from that place but that place energy also was not ready to leave me. What a deep connection! What a deep relation! Shiv... Shiv...Shiv...

I had a great desire to stay at that place, I wanted to stay there, but anyhow we moved ahead. We took Bhog-Prasad and continued our journey through Jageshwar Dham, Neem Karoli Babaji's Ashram.

We then moved towards Jageshwar Dham which is close to Almora. My sister and I were the only women in the car and it was 8:00 at night. A lot of work was being done on the way in the mountains. I had decided in my mind that as soon as 8:00 pm strikes, we would stop our cars and would not go further. It was about to be 8 o'clock, we were about to reach near Almora but Jageshwar Dham was still visible at a distance of a few kilometers. I told my friends that if we meet anyone on the way, we would ask them for directions to Jageshwar Dham, and if not, we would decide what to do next. In the darkness of the night, we saw two policemen.

We asked one of them if there was any hotel or ashram nearby as we were heading towards Jageshwar Dham. We stopped at 8:00 p.m. A policeman was there said, *"Go Ahead, don't be panic."* It seemed as if we got a divine signal and we moved ahead. That was a sign for us from God Himself. As soon as we turned our direction towards Jageshwar Dham, it was a wonderful sight. It was a wonderful bright night.

We did not know that on these mountains that day was celebrated as a festival. It was the day of Ekadashi, which was celebrated as Dev Diwali in the mountains of Almora. Thousands of Diyas were everywhere.

The entire mountain was filled with Diwali lights. There were lamps in the courtyard of every house. Surprisingly, the dark night turned out to be Diwali. The only light on the entire route was the light of lamps and candles. In this way it seemed that the supreme powers were calling us, the powers of Mahadev or Bhole Baba about which Mahavatar Babaji had given me the hint earlier. We reached quite late at night. Everything was closed all around. All the hotels were closing. We opted for one of the hotels, had dinner and rested for the night. Jageshwar Temple is a Hindu pilgrimage. It is one of the Dhams in the Shaivism tradition.

It must have been at least 3:20 or 3:30 in the morning, while sleeping, I suddenly started hearing a very loud sound of bells. I woke up hearing the sound of bells and I asked my sister, *"Can you also hear any sound?"* She said, *"No, I can't hear anything."* I felt as if someone was calling me.

I took one of my friends with me and we headed towards the temple. It was 4:30 in the morning. It was almost dark. We started walking towards the temple. We could not even see the entrance of the temple. There was no one in the temple, only a few dogs were sitting on the road, some were lying down. I started calling out, *"Is someone there? Please tell us when the temple will open."* After about 10 minutes, a priest came by the temple and said, there is still time for the temple to open.

After some time, the doors of the temple opened and we entered inside. When we went inside, a very beautiful incident happened. Here I want to tell you one thing, I am in contact with Mahavatar Babaji, sometimes in his Shiva form, sometimes in his own form. I have had many experiences with them in this life. Whatever he told and conveyed is as follows.

We reached Jageshwar Dham early in the morning. We called Pandit ji and he told me to wake up Lord Shiva because it is Dev Uthani Ekadashi. The Gods who were sleeping now had to be woken up from their sleep on this Ekadashi and it was the time to start all the auspicious works.

What a moment! Moment of joy, bliss and full of gratitude. There was no limit to the happiness in my mind, Lord Shiva, the one who awakened this world, his divine live energy was present there, in this material world and it was such a great privilege of mine that I was removing the curtain to awaken Him. I was ringing this bell to wake Him up. I was feeling extremely blessed.

Although I did not do much worship, rituals etc. in my life, except on special occasions. But on that day, I felt that today I should perform Rudrabhishek. For the first time after Dev Uthani Ekadashi, I became a participant in conducting Rudrabhishek at Jageshwar Dham. In this way our devotion to Jageshwar Dham was completed and it was a very beautiful experience.

After that, we headed towards dwarahat to visit Mahavatar Babaji Cave. By the time we reached, it was 3:00 in the afternoon. I met all the people of my Sangha at Kukuchina and sent them to climb for Babaji's cave.

I was getting messages from Mahavatar Babaji that I had to come alone in the cave but I was going with the Sangh. Again and again, I was getting messages to come alone. In this way, during this one visit, Babaji called for darshan twice in his cave. That day I went with everyone in a group.

When I went along with the entire Sangh at Babaji's cave, we meditated. It was evening while we were meditating in the cave. Everyone was feeling divine feelings and were also having very good experiences.

As soon as I sat to meditate in the cave, I felt that Yukteshwar Giri Ji Maharaj and Lahiri Mahasaya Ji were sitting at the entrance of the cave and Mahavatar Babaji was coming towards the cave walking with very fast steps and repeating the same words again and again. The words were repeated – LOK KALYAN KARYA, LOK KALYAN KARYA. (Service for mankind)

I felt that Babaji wanted this work to be done very urgently and we have to do service for Lok Kalayan very quickly. And after that Babaji sat in the cave for some time.

At night we all, more than 28 soul sisters did meditation with fire element in the form of bonfire. Everyone received messages. At that time, Babaji gave the message to work very quickly by spreading and propagating this knowledge in the society and in the world. Babaji was talking about the awakening of consciousness. The awakening of self-layer, when a human work with the awakened self and understand herself or himself more fully above body and mind, the next step is in connecting with the I AM, connecting with the divine soul.

The next morning when we went to Babaji's cave, I had to go there completely alone but there were one or two people with me. When I was going in the morning, instead of going towards the cave, I turned towards such a path, where Babaji along with his troupe had performed Yagya along with Yukteshwar Giri Ji Maharaj, Lahiri Mahasaya Ji and Yogananda Ji. Looking at the fresh ashes of that yagya, it seemed as if a yagya had just been performed. We were surprised. We also stayed there for some time and performed a Yagya and offered some twigs from nearby areas as an offering in that Yagya. The heart was filled with immense love, reverence and devotion.

That day in the cave with Babaji, I again received the same message - to impart this knowledge to the entire world. This Kriya Yoga knowledge has to be shared among everyone. This path of Kriya Yoga, which is described in the Geeta, has to be given to everyone and everyone has to be made aware of it.

Planet Earth Energies are shifting; everyone's energy has to shift. Shift in each consciousness matters for planetary shift. When a human being starts expressing and experiencing his life through his soul, they will have the grand wisdom to choose and express their life with love, joy, compassion and giving.

In this way our great journey moves forward towards perfection. I got the opportunity to impart this knowledge at a college in Dwarahat. The students were initiated into meditation for two days and received teachings on meditation.

☆☆☆

Thus now in our journey we moved towards Asha Pyramid and meditated there. Asha Pyramid is at Dunagiri Retreat. We all soul sisters and soul brothers met Piyushji. We meditated in the divine energies of Babaji and the Pyramid. After that we left for Rishikesh where there was a program of Dhyan Mahotsav. We reached there at 2:30 in the night. Next morning, I joined Patri Ji in the morning meditation session.

Another very strange incident happened. One Meditator laughed at me and mocked me in the name of Mahavatar Babaji and said something like, you have come here after visiting the cave of Mahavatar Babaji. When you will not be here on planet in your physical form, A cave will be built in your name also and everyone will go to see your cave too just like Babaji's Cave.

They said such harsh words which brought tears to my eyes and I went and sat on the banks of Mother Ganga with tears in my eyes.

What does it mean *"My cave"* after my lifetime - What a mockery of me? What is this? I closed my eyes. As soon as I closed my eyes, Mahavatar Babaji was in front of me.

I could hear his words very clearly. He said, *"Don't mourn, don't even be sad. What you are considering as a joke or a ridicule is going to be the reality. You are a follower of my tradition of Kriya Yoga. You have come into this world to show the path of truth to many and when this work is completed then people will know you. Do not mourn"*

I was into ecstasy state. I was greeted by the cheerful words of Mahavatar Babaji, visible or invisible tears turned into Pearls of Joy. That time I felt a deeper connection of duality. How the birth of light lit in the womb of darkness. This is a perishable existence with dual characteristics but we are the seers, witnessing the whole drama. I am that truth, that soul who is forever. I felt so balanced now, there is no emotional charge for situations and experiences within myself or with others.

I felt a sense of complete acceptance, whatever is happening. Balance is a consciousness in which you feel complete with yourself, you feel complete in your circumstances and you feel complete in your situations.

Thank you Babaji!

10 CLEANSING THE SOUL

One day suddenly I received a message from Babaji that I have to invite everyone to meditate this evening at my meditation center, *"May I Help You"*. This Pyramid Meditation Center was built in the basement area of my house. I was wondering who would come on such short notice?

Because I received Babaji's message in the morning and if I send a message now then how will people be able to come by evening at such short notice. Since it was Babaji's message, I had to do it with full faith and complete surrender. I created a message and shared it in all the groups. In the evening, I went to my meditation center and sat in meditation.

After some time, I saw that no one had come, the entire meditation center was empty. Smiling in my mind, I opened my eyes a couple of times to see if anyone was there, but there was no one. I smiled and started whispering with Babaji, *"Babaji! you have said that meditation session has to be held, people will come but no one has come."* I again started meditating and in my meditation experience, I started clearing seeing that now the place of center in the basement area was completely filling. Consciousnesses were continuously arriving and the entire space was filled.

I amazed to visualize, whatever consciousnesses were coming, were not in the physical forms. They did not have a physical or gross body. They were all in non – physical forms. After some time Mahavatar Babaji and Yukteshwar Giri Ji came and sat on one side. On one side everyone and on the opposite side Mahavatar Babaji and Guru Ji. I want all readers to be part of the journey, of course this is my experience, but if you become its part then you will ascend. Babaji and Guruji gave me a signal to witness.

Suddenly, while meditating, what I see is that a action started happening on all those bodies. With two colours liquid, I could see some energies were taking place on them. I can definitely tell that their veins and nerves were being activated by blue and red colours. It was similar as blood flows in human bodies. When you align with the Creator, Miracles do happen.

Babaji and Guru Yukteshwer ji were teaching me through live demonstration of the process. As soon as that energy reached in their hearts, the process was completed. I questioned Babaji, whether this process which was happening now, are the energies yet to go to the upper bodies. Babaji told me only these words. This process was enough for today, the rest will be later.

Right now this was enough for these consciousnesses. In this way, initiation was given by Babaji that when we are in Sadhana, how we work not only with the physical bodies, human beings but also with non physical beings too. The spirits living on the earth and who are not on the physical form even though they are on the earth. These are the Earth bond souls. How does the consciousness of those who are not visible, who are not physical, change? I witnessed a completely strange process and received an initiation in a completely strange way. How you leave planet earth has a big effect on next life time.

Babaji spoke about my job to serve these kinds of souls. He told this is astral service and we work with earth energies and cosmic energies too. Even if you are in physical form, you can still work on your spiritual levels. The remembrance of many life time experiences may be covered in dust, just as it is this time.

Trust your Masters, invite all your soul layers or soul, then in the presence of Babaji and Yukteshwer ji cleanse. Cleansing is just blending of energy. Babaji's pure energies are present. Breathe in these love energies. Feel with your imagination that your heart is joining with a pure green light, tinged with gold. Kindly breathe into it.

That day Babaji was in a huge form.

Thank you Babaji!

11 PARAMHANS YOGANANDAJI'S HOUSE VISIT

In 2018, I planned to go to Kolkata for four-five days because my maternal grandmother had passed away. It was my second day in Kolkata. I was going somewhere on the road. All of the sudden, I received a message from Babaji that I have to go to Yogananda's house today. Yes, I knew that he had a house in Kolkata, but I am not knowing where is it, how can I go, whom I should talk to and what is this sign?

I prayed Babaji to arrange all the things and this incident was around two in the afternoon. Within five mins of prayer my eyes caught the right side of the road on which there was some information about Yogananda society or Kriya yoga written, which I do not remember completely right now.

I was happy because now I had the means to reach Yogananda Ji place. I quickly asked the driver to stop the car and went inside the office where flyer was there. I enquired about Yogananda Ji house, person I need to contact and details of visit. A person informed me that no one can go to Yogananda Ji house without appointment and no visiting hours post 5pm in the evening. But the Babaji's voice inside me was insisting me to go to Yogananda Ji house by today and to go alone.

I requested in office that, I need to contact the person in charge today only since I had come from outside Kolkata and my return flight was next day early morning. After so many request, I got the contact number. I called the number and was delighted to know it was Yogananda ji's brother's son, who runs the ashram and lives in the house. I request him to give permission to visit the place and it was message from Babaji's. He asked me to come around five in the evening. There was no limit to my happiness. I had time. I completed rest of the work and was ready to visit Premavatar Yogananda ji's house. In an instant, weather changed. It stared raining very heavily.

I went as the per the direction received to reach the house. The car stopped in front of Yogananda Ji house. As soon as I saw that house, a tingling sensation and a lightning flashed through my whole body. The main door of the house was closed.

I dialed the number, the door opened and I entered. The door was locked back. There was no one else inside but one person and that was Yogananda's own favourite person. He started giving me tour of the place. The place where Yogananda Ji sat, the place where Yukteswar Giri Ji used to come and sit, the same chair, the same picture, everything was as if it was alive.

It seemed as if everything was saying something and finally, we went to the third floor of the house.

There was a seat in a small room where Yogananda Ji used to meditate. I got permission to sit at that place. I sat there and started meditating. I started feeling the presence of Mahavatar Babaji. He was in front of me. He was very happy and we had some conversation which cannot be disclosed here.

I was very happy with the experience. Later when I came down, I saw a woman in front of me who appeared to be his wife. Both of us introduced ourselves and we chatted for some time. After spending about two hours at Yogananda Ji's house, I took leave from there. With a very beautiful experience of silence and again a deep peace with Babaji's energies.

Thank you Babaji!

12 EXPANDING THE CONSCIOUSNESS

Somewhere I got a message from Mahavatar Babaji that there was a pull towards going to America. As if some power or some consciousness is calling me there again and again. In the physical existence on earth, Brahmarishi Patri Ji had also told me many times to go to America, that people are waiting there and you have to go there to spread meditation. This was a great surprise for me, but it was also a matter of faith.

It was the year 2016, time was passing slowly and I too kept thinking in my mind that whoever is calling, we are ready to come. You make our arrangements and we are ready to come. In this way, with passing time our program was finalised by 2018. After all, we had planned to go there but couldn't even think of which direction to go first. That time Mahavatar Babaji energies emerged with whole information. Babaji started instructing me where and how to go. The first place he chose was Los Angeles.

Our family have to go there first. I still remember that day when I reached Los Angeles. Babaji assured me that I am with you here also. All this work is being done under my direction. I was surprised and felt happy that my entire life's divine purpose is being guided by Babaji. Our whole visit was around more for more than fifty days. We went to thirteen cities and was amazed that most of them were near Self Realization Fellowship (SRF). As soon as we reached there, we took some rest and went out for a tour.

The next day, we wandered through on the streets of Hollywood. It was very surprising that there was something lying on the road of Hollywood. There was a white glove lying in a corner of the road in Baba Mudra on the sparkling clean streets amidst tall shiny buildings.

I was surprised the moment I saw the glove on the road. I immediately felt as if it was saying something to me. I felt Babaji's presence so far away in the air as if Babaji himself had called me. Expressing a lot of gratitude, we spent our whole day in different studios and various demonstration sites there.

Suddenly, while roaming around at a place, a desire arose in my mind that Yogananda's ashram is also here. In this way, such a situation was created that I could reach and see that place. It was a holy place where SRF was born. Peaceful, calm and serene on the top of the hill. The views were absolutely spectacular.

We stayed in America for two months and kept feeling the energy there at different places. Ashrams of the Yogananda Satsang Society were everywhere. There was such joy and peace within, Mahavatar Babaji said that Kriya Yoga would spread in all lands.

☆☆☆

This journey was not like I had to preach or educate anyone. There was a secret desire to go there and connect because there was someone calling. This whole mystery was revealed when we reached California, San Francisco.

We were staying in a guest house there. From there, we had to go to Mount Shasta. Mount Shasta, an ice – capped volcano in Northern California, is a popular destination for spiritual seekers. It is known for its healing properties and spiritual energy. Our train tickets and stay were also booked. Later, on our travel dates, the train service was stopped as repair work was going on the tracks. Therefore, it was not possible to reach Mount Shasta by train.

We had to cancel the program to go there. Now, we have to stay in San Francisco for the next five days. suddenly, there was some change in the behavior of the owner of the guest house where we were staying. We requested her to stay there for few more days as we could not decide on any further plans. But the owner told us that she has to go somewhere and we can't stay there any longer.

We requested her but she did not agree. On the other hand, we had hotel reservations in Mount Shasta. Finally, we decided to leave that place. Nature itself pulled us there. Even though we were saying no, the place called us there.

We travelled by bus and arrived at Mount Shasta. We began to feel a completely different type of divine energy. Such an energy as if everything here is talking, a different energy. We went to many places there and I could feel that there were many different activities happening. It was as if nature was speaking at the place of the hot water spring. There is one another place in Mount Shasta called the *"Seat of God"*. We had a guide there. It seemed as if there was something inside the earth. That place is called *"Ascension Rock"*.

We reached the place in the evening which was surrounded by white snow mountains. We were on a path that led towards the mountain towards the peaks and valleys, which seemed as if we were on the earth and were also entering another dimension. It seemed like a place with a very different energy.

As soon as we got down there, we saw a board on which was written *"Kriya Yoga."* I was wondering which place in the world is this where there is Kriya

Yoga retreat. There were some people who had come for training and were moving forward after training. The rest of the space was empty. There was no one there. It seemed as if a camp was set up there. There was a single person who was doing some cleaning on the table. He was also busy with his work.

The time was 5:30 in the evening. Some small mountains were visible in the front. We started sitting there. Our guide was with us as well. As soon as we reached there, I had a mystical experience with my open eyes. It seemed as if three stairs had fallen down in front of us from the sky, just like the stairs are in a circus, made of thin threads.

There were three of us – me, Gupta ji and Devika. Only three stairs fell down from the top. We got the message, *"You are ready for Ascension. Get on these stairs. The stairs have come for you. You are here now because you have arrived."* After this experience, I remembered Mahavatar Babaji. It felt like, yes, this is why I was being called to America. It is Mount Shasta energies that I was drawn to while living in Delhi, India.

Mountains were visible all around. It felt like there was a special mountain that I had to sit on. The place started changing again and again as to which hill we had to sit on. Some believe that the mountain is home to the creator and some believe that the mountain is a portal to the metaphysical world.

Suddenly, through telepathy, we felt that this was the mountain for us, where all three of us had to be.

As soon as we sat on that mountain, all three of us started having different types of experiences. It seemed as if people had come out from under the earth to welcome us. We were meeting them and they were very happily shouting at each other and saying, look! They have come, hey look, they have come. They were putting garlands around our necks. They were very happy. Those beings, our soul brothers and sisters, were very happy. They were talking from the place which was below our feet. They were calling us, *"We are honored to give you a message. We will talk about the Ascension Rock, one of the favorite meeting places where many of our Council meetings convey.*

Beneath this space and beneath these bundles that you touch, lie one of our temples where we sit and discuss many topics related to earth ascension and to our emergence to the surface. When you come here and sit quietly, we often pull you in our meetings and you become one of our members representing the surface spokesman and your input is most valuable.

It is at this time that we truly merge with one voice representing the population of one Earth. Our voice from below and yours from above. It is this merging of perceptions that help us for our plans and from our forthcoming tracks to the surface in the very near future. This will be a monumental step on our part and one we have envisioned and planned for a very long time and now the time is here.

What Joy is in our hearts to finally put our plan into action and make our way to the surface through our tunnel entrances that have already existed. Our tunnels are underground which have been secured and we have never been exposed to anything like this. We were waiting for you. We know everyone who comes here to this mountain. As soon as you started climbing this mountain here, we recognised you. As you set out to climb Mount Shasta, the spirit of Mount Shasta will identify you.

The mountain has that spirit of shasta. It picks up your vibration and knows who you are and exactly where you are as you walk along its path. Nothing is hidden from it. It heard your voices and recorded your thoughts and registered your movements. So, talk to the mountain. I am always eager to converse with you."

The message continued, *"Our auras of light embrace you in our Energy field and we will merge together as one soul representing Earth's diverse family."*

"What a blessing it is for us when you are here, when you stand on this spot. We are most, most honored to join our hearts with your awakening

hearts. For instance, you are just a foot above us but in our heart space there is no distance between us. We become merged as one heart when you stand above. When you stand above us, you become a patron of light and your light is magnified ten folds as together-together in this secret spot.

You shine as a spotlight as our light from below will be focused into your light from above and it radiates out blessings for all lives on the planet. This is the force of light that we gather together as one.

So, gather together as much as you can, whether in your home or outdoors for this exponentially increase of your light quotient in waves. Bless all those in your localities. Soon our people will be emerging from our homes. We need those hands and we will greet you in your homes and embrace you in our arms and we will become one together as one family, one beacon of light broadcasting our Unity out to the universe. At last, we are filled with gratitude when your presence is here and trees bow to you in welcome and the mountain itself. The spirit of Shasta is deeply honored when you all are standing on its ground. What a day of celebration."

Our meditation experience was kind of a story. Those people were Lemurians. They were higher dimensional beings. Like the legends say, Lemurians date back thousands of years, even to the time of Atlantis.

We were surrounded by a loving, nurturing and positive environment. We had consciously created this for ourselves. So, as we have created that divine light from Mount Shasta, he told me that, *"Even you can do that. We are from thousands of days back. As we have done, even you can do so.*

You can invite that light, you can invite that wisdom, you can invite those knowing and the knowledge to understand the laws. You can do that. So very soon you will find yourself living among those who are wise and nurturing."

Yes, of course, for those beings who have chosen less, they will be separated from you and sent to a much lower dimensional world. They will choose themselves. *"So, we have come to a place where you have to choose. Come, all of you, join us, because now our journey is together, because we have already evolved and we are evolving and working for Mother Earth. As light workers you are also working for Mother Earth. So, we are praying for your success and it is God's plan."*

They told me it's always been that way. In a way this is the arrival of Christ, the arrival of light. *"Please do not underestimate yourselves, as all of you Light Workers carry the Christ Consciousness in your souls. You are Christ and you have come again into the Christ energies incarnated on planet Earth where they can permeate all life forms. So, please don't underestimate yourself, don't look at others and don't pray to others to change your life. It is your duty to change your life. And please, don't be afraid either. Reclaim your divinity. My dear soul brothers and sisters, this is for you."*

The most beautiful part was that they were also speaking like dear soul brothers and sisters. So, I believe that light, that consciousness who connected with me was my soul brother only because it was the voice of a male. So, he said, *"Yes, of course and we are permitting you. We give your strength. We give you light daily. We give you chords of unlimited love. Just focus there. Just make a connection with that. We awake your consciousness connections to us for the time where you will be permitted to visit us here in Telos.*

Then, we will truly become one light, shining from Earth for all the cosmos to witness our love radiating into the in the galaxy in a magnificent display of light. "We all are light. We all are love. We use our divinity to navigate, to speak our soul purpose for incarnating. We use our divinity to steer us into the right direction of our soul paths of greater and greater heights. As we are greater beings. One day you will also be very much like this only because you all are also light workers."

This is the end time. All souls whoever incarnated on planet Earth have returned. This end time can be met with harmony and joy or fear and chaos. The choice is yours. We recommend you turn your focus towards God while our feet walk on Earth, for God is in full command of everything and you all are in his hands. So, this is the cosmic thing that we are.

We all are traveling to higher and higher consciousness until we meet on planes of reality, we are all glisters with a golden sheer of God's light. We all are traveling with you. We are traveling with you on this trip to the stars. *"My dear soul brothers we are where our thoughts take us and if our thoughts are lofty, we find ourselves in heaven. So be here and be now. We can see each other's light. What is important at this time is to ignore the darkness and not let the fear enter your aura. Please don't allow the fears to enter into your aura. Stay blessed. Think only of the light that your great Godself is always flooding into your being. Stay safe always in the protective shields of light that is always around you. Let others experience their own journeys. For yours is to bring forth our message from us."*

So, this was a beautiful collective message. The message that what is our purpose in life and what we are exactly doing. These are the ascension plans and this is for everyone. We are here and you are on the planet earth.

This is such a wonderful message and when I was receiving these messages, I was just being witness to something very near, to somewhat somewhere what is happening in the bright light of Babaji's only.

I felt as if whatever magical world was happening, was happening in front of me and dazzling me. I felt like a new construction was going on. The old is going and the new is coming. I somehow felt that the light of all the divine masters who are working for this universe were falling upon me. We felt like we were on this side and they were on that side but Babaji's good feelings gave me full confidence that new seeds are being sown on the earth. That time has now come. That thing was being shown to me by calling me so far away. It was amazing.

I live in the far north of India, but I felt Mahavatar Babaji's power in the way he gave me the message he has to give to the entire earth, which has been directed to come in the form of a book. That's why I salute Babaji. Thank you Babaji again and again from the bottom of my heart.

In this way, we stayed at Mount Shasta for three-four days and received messages from the energies there. I didn't feel like returning from that place at all. Returning back with new energy, we set out for New York. Everything was happening very amazingly on the trip to America.

In New York, I got to see and visit the Yogoda Satsanga Society too. After that we stayed in America for 20-25 days in which we went to Columbus, Washington DC, Niagara Falls. Even in Niagara Falls, when I got connected with nature, I was seeing Mahavatar Babaji everywhere.

It seemed as if Canada was also inviting me. In this way it seemed as if some harmony was taking place. I am feeling very overwhelmed in my heart. I am feeling this type of vibration in my heart that

Mahavatar Babaji, entering the fifth dimension, is alerting us as to how we have to move forward and with what kind of new energies we have to understand.

Thank you Babaji!

13 INVOKING OF DIVINE FEMININE CONSCIOUSNESS

It was 14th April 2020. Babaji woke me up early in the morning and called me to another room. I felt that Babaji called me, there must be an important message. Somewhere Babaji was pointing towards a word. A letter *"W"* was appearing to me again and again. It seemed as if Babaji was talking about the word *"woman"*.

Babaji was giving a message through light language. Babaji was indicating that the time now had come. That day Babaji did not come alone, he came with Mother Adishakti. I was surprised and thought that today Adishakti Maa has also come with Babaji. Babaji was saying that the time has come for the divine feminine energy to awaken, that's why you have to start *"World Women Mystics and Goddesses."* You have to talk about Feminine energies. He was pointing towards women empowerment.

At first, I found it strange to talk about women goddess as we were only talking about meditation and pyramids. After that Babaji revealed the whole secret. For two-three days the energies of Babaji and Maa Adishakti remained at my place and they said that the earth is going through a phase of transformation.

In it, an introduction about goddesses, women mystics and women saints is to be given. In this, not only the Indian goddesses but also the goddesses of the whole world were pointed out. Then he also talked about re-awakening the energies of different places of the seven continents which had disappeared over time. He wanted me to talk about it on the Pyramid Live channel. When I asked him for how many days this program would continue, he said, *"You keep going. You will be informed."* This program ran three times for twenty-one days each and the total was sixty-four.

Babaji and Adishakti Maa said that it was a very special time, when a great spiritual transformation was taking place in the entire earth. The shift of consciousness is masculine and feminine energies so both of them had come together at the same time. That is, the divine Goddess powers and the Adi Dev element, the sky element. He said that these divine feminine powers have to be reawakened. This awakening energy of all Goddess will hold the earth, so that all people can be healed properly. You can also ask to transmit the energies with its true purpose into the different codes in your body, you all have 144 sacred codes to be activated.

Babaji was talking about wounded female energies to be cleared and healed. Everyone has to recognize their divinity. We all have taken birth for this divine purpose. You have been chosen at this time to awaken these divine powers. You need to talk. Small groups have to be formed so that man can be freed from his negative thoughts. Those energies in the form of spiritual experiences of humans will help them to transform negative thoughts. To heal them and connect them to their Higher Self so that their consciousnesses can be nourished. I felt very fortunate to have been chosen for this divine work.

All this work was done and I told all this to Patri Sir also. My language had also suddenly changed. I started calling everyone *"My dear soul brothers and sisters"*. A change took place in my house also. The energies changed in my house as I walked. Patri Sir said, *"These divine energies have chosen you for their work and the "White Brotherhood" will now function like the "White Sisterhood"*. The task will be to help the inhabitants of the earth. In this way a new name was found which was born by Patri Sir.

We chose different speakers to speak about the divine energies chosen during this event. This includes Mother Isis, Mother Mary, Sekhmet's energies, Greek, Russian, South African, American Goddesses. Behind all these Goddesses I could sense only Adishakti energies which were there in every Goddess form. The Goddesses said that the lower three chakras of all human beings had been blocked for many years. They were in mutual differences. Work has to be done to free people from their emotional problems, otherwise it will take a lot of time for these chakras to awaken. This is how I came to know about different tasks.

The energies of Mahavatar Babaji told that the time has come. Brahma started the Vedas and mantras of Adishakti Maa with the energies of purity. The science of reciting and expressing the mantras of the Vedas developed gradually. With time all these powers had become impure. People gradually got trapped in the web of their material wealth and all those powers got distributed by using different spiritual rules. Here again, the male and female elements were equally strong but now Devi Shakti realized that the male dominated religions in the world had made themselves more powerful.

So, the Goddesses extinct themselves from the world and Lord Vishnu incarnated to rule this

Kaliyuga. The era gradually started descending in its pace. In this fifth dimension, it can be said that many divine powers are reawakening which is also the last phase of Kaliyuga.

This is the reason that these energies are coming before us, which are the energies of Mother Saraswati, Parvati, Gayatri, Isis and the energies of Mother Mary. The tolerance of this truth and love through the different energies of Sekhmet will be reestablished. Those creative powers, the yin and yang energies or the male and female energies, will all be in balance again. In this way I saw that through the beginning of *"World Women Mystics and Goddesses"* a new transformation of consciousness taking place within everyone. There was a tremendous change in the lives of all the speakers who came to speak.

Now let's talk about those women artists and litterateurs. Artists have been influenced by different energies at different times, given us energy in the form of their art paintings. Writers also gave energy through their writings. Whenever a woman is born as a politician or an artist, she has to struggle a lot. She takes the challenges of her life and moves ahead in the world and gives new knowledge to the world.

So, the whole change is required for the ascension of Planet Earth's` shift. Our Earth is called Mother

Earth, she nurtures and supports humanity and life. Mother Earth is a unified field of male and female.

Thank you Babaji!

14 COMMUNICATION WITH NATURE AND ANIMAL GODS

Man considers himself too limited to shift the consciousness of the Earth for the fifth dimension. Along with the awakening of feminine energies, Babaji was also giving me some other messages after some days. He was giving me knowledge about communication. He said, *"You have powers through which you can connect with anyone, communicate with anyone in unlimited ways. You have the powers of communication and telepathy."*

I received the emergence of knowledge of these new powers within me. Babaji told me that I can establish communication with anyone. It may be animal, nature or anyone around me because the entire earth is Vasudev Kutumbakam. Express your pure intension to attune yourself and must tell to Mother Earth that your highest intention is to align with her so that you may experience more. I was initiated to awaken these abilities by interacting with the energies of air, earth, water, fire, stars, constellations, animals, snakes, lions and elephants for three months. The elements can support people tremendously in raising their consciousness. Nature gave messages. The question came to my mind: should we write *"Animal God"*. I received the answer that they are also divine, their energies are also divine. So, we kept this word. Our new series begin with the name - Communication with Animal Gods.

Babaji made me a channel, I started giving this wisdom to the world and started saying that when we talk to any other consciousness, connect with them, a connection is formed between us, through this connection our communication starts. The consciousness then gives us a message and indicates something. We also have an educational relationship with them through which we keep developing further.

During this fifth dimensional transition we will be in such a high vibration that we will be able to understand more. We will be able to hear and see much more. We have to understand them all. The time is about to come when people from other planets will establish relations with us. Then, without hesitation, we can consider them our brothers and sisters and give them respect. We and the nature are the same. We already have five elements within us. Our own elements speak with elements of nature.

Communication is a vital part of life and living. It is an act or process of sharing or exchanging of thoughts, opinions or information. It also refers to something imparted, interchanged or transmitted. In general, it refers to the use of speech or written words, as is done through verbal or written messages from person to person.

Communication also refers to passing on an emotion. We often hear of people conveying their feelings not through vocal or verbal messages, but by their sheer presence. Sharing of intimate thoughts and feelings influence all human beings. Communication is not restricted only to human beings. It is equally important to plants and animals.

Effective communication depends upon two individuals, one who is communicating the information and the other who receives the information. It is important that the communicator who communicates the information must do it in a way that is understood and acceptable to the other one. However, if the other person is unable to understand the information or is not willing to accept it, the communication becomes ineffective.

Telepathy is the sending and receiving of thought messages, mental and emotional states, consciously or unconsciously by means of what may be called *"the sixth sense"* of the physical plane. It is the communication of impressions of any kind from one mind to another, independently of the recognised channels of sense.

In addition to the five physical senses of man, there were also two other physical senses, comparatively underdeveloped in the average person and one of them is the telepathic sense.

Telepathy is the mental process by which *"one knows at a distance."* The sending and receiving of currents and waves of feelings and thoughts. The term itself has been usually used in the sense of deliberate and conscious sending and receiving of thought and feeling waves. There is a much wider field of phenomena covered by it.

The scientific authority has accepted the phenomenon of telepathy. It is not considered in the realm of the uncanny or supernatural. So, telepathy is intangible reality. It is basically the action of our mind on another's at a distance and without means of the senses.

☆☆☆

Babaji gave me this idea that you have to speak about communication because communication is really fundamental to existence and it is not only the existence of human beings, it is also a process of creating and sharing information. This communication can take place from anyone to anyone, between man with man, with the five elements, with animals, with nature, with the moon and stars. There will be only one purpose for doing this - to share ideas so that we can think, understand, share viewpoints and we can also share facts.

A person must learn this today so that he can know how to live better in this world. Babaji says that this communication always happens between two consciousnesses. In communication there is always a message sender and a message receiver. On one side there is someone who gives the message and someone else receives that message. The one who is sending the message initiates the message and is also its source.

For example, If I want to communicate with a water element, I will start talking about the water element first. In this way, I have started sending the messages. Then further communication begins. The message has got its direction. Let's say today I receive a message from a fish, then I will accept it as a message from a fish.

Whatever message is coming, that message is decoded. The message generated by the sender is symbolically encoded in form of words, images or gestures. This is a way in which messages can be transmitted throughs our meditation or telepathically, verbally or by mental images. So, the message is carried by that media.

Babaji says that we have the power to send our message to anyone. The recipient of the message will reply back when he receives the message and when he is able to understand the message. Hence, if I communicate to the water element, it will also reply and send me a message.

If any obstructions that are caused by the sender, then message are not received during the process of communication. For example, if we are unable to establish contact due to our low frequency, the message will not be able to get through. If we are not able to communicate, it means that we have not established contact with each other.

☆☆☆

We can understand this easily. I feel that this remote sensing conversation can also be called telepathy. This is being done by human brain waves. Babaji's words behind this were like the waves in the calm mind of the human being, which we also call telepathy, different messages suitable to our aura are sent to different areas of the receptors through telepathy. The calmer we are, the better we can receive the messages sent through telepathy. We also see that these messages which are sent through telepathy are coming in through our receptive brain and it is receiving them.

Many people have this knowledge. Babaji meant by this was that we humans do not know our given potential. We have to use this ability. Therefore, this ability needs to be learned by everyone communicated to everyone. For this reason, the program of *"Communication with Nature and Animal Gods"* was launched on our YouTube channel, Asha Foundation -Adishakti, and on our Facebook page, Pyramid Light. Different masters were invited to introduce this subject. If all those masters can experience them, why can't we all. In those 21 days of workshops, it was found that we can talk and take the messages from other beings.

The intuition which a person receives is given to him by other consciousness which is received by him. This is a kind of specialty of the feminine element. We are moving towards the Earth's changing consciousness, towards the fifth dimension, towards higher consciousnesses.

Therefore, whether it is a man or a woman, this power will have to awaken within him. This has to be practiced by everyone. It has to be understood and it is also necessary for the inhabitants of the earth. They need to be receptive so that other consciousnesses that want to give messages to the Earth's inhabitants can send the messages, and they can understand them, evolve and by expanding their consciousness can also develop the Earth's consciousness. The most important thing is the development of Earth's consciousness. Development of all of us means development of the earth.

We have to understand our capabilities, experiment with it and understand. We need to develop our communication skills to see how this happens. Different mediums are being created for communication. Other inhabitants of the other planets and extra terrestrial beings are also preparing to establish communication with us. Grids of higher planets, other realms, other energies are being prepared for us to receive messages by communicating with us.

There are some messages that are being given to us by their own higher consciousnesses. There are some message networks that are being given only to us. There are some messages that are being given to many people where everyone can talk. There are some messages where the higher consciousness is simply giving messages to the higher consciousness. There are some messages that are received only when we are ready, some people have this characteristic that they take the messages of nature very quickly. They are very sensitive.

There are some people who are able to receive messages from particular persons or from other things. Some people are sensitive towards animals and are able to take their messages. But the important thing is to take the message and understand that I have the power within me to take this message.

☆☆☆

That is the reason why Babaji repeatedly said that this has to be said to the people of the earth. Babaji chose me for this work. He said, *"You can do it"*, so this project was given to me. The earth is changing a lot. This is to send the people of Earth about what we need - sending messages and receiving messages. For both these things we all have to be prepared and practice for it.

When I started learning the communication process through this workshop, I found out how conversation can be done. I also shared many experiences of my life.

By communicating we saw how we can interact with animals. They have the ability to be our animal guides as well. If we are able to talk to them then they are mostly showing us our problems and they are trying to show us the problems of our life in some form or the other and also tell us the solutions. If they understand both the internal and external circumstances of a person, they also tell the right solution. If we talk to animals then they will definitely tell us the solutions to our problems.

When we try to have a conversation with nature, then we can imagine that we are having a conversation with the ocean. Even a man becomes a child by going near the sea. The sea has water which is salty. The sea also has healing abilities as it eliminates negative energy. The sea completely cures not only physical but also mental diseases, fear, anxiety and worries within us.

☆☆☆

If we become one with our breath and calm our mind, our thoughts and emotions are becoming still and then we establish contact with the water. We see all the problems leaving our consciousness and interact with it. We can send messages also. This process of establishing communication is possible only when we have completely calmed ourselves.

When consciousness starts flowing in a completely void state, we connect to a place where we are connected to nature and observe it and then we become sensitive. Whatever our situation is at that time, the way we connect with nature, be it forest goddess, nature goddess, we are able to establish communication with them and through communication it shows us the way.

Babaji had also given the same message that by connecting with our heart chakra, our Shiva Shakti, the energies within us, gives us powers. There are limitless powers in nature and we can all use them.

We discussed communication here, we can also communicate with our energy bodies after our death. Whatever spirits are there and whatever is non-living, they are also a part of us. This means that these powers are preparing us for the upcoming changes on Earth. A new world will become available to us through a new perspective where we are able to understand, we are able to communicate and we are able to understand our psychic abilities.

Thank you Babaji!

15 SHIVOHAM

Many messages are being given by Mahavtar Babaji, Angels, Saint German and Masters of DNA all around the earth to help humanity and their ascension. Babaji is giving us messages to be prepared. If we receive the messages, are we able to understand it? Will everyone be able to decode them and understand them?

Therefore, we are being instructed to be prepared with our full awareness and knowledge. Having deposited energy and upliftment, we can understand the meaning of receiving messages from anyone. Decoding, the most important ability in the communication process.

We are connecting with the God, Goddess, Babaji, Masters, ETS and we are flowing with energies, getting the codes, symbolic languages, other means and decoding is going at the same time. If nature wants to connect with us or any natural element, animal world, bird world, other planets or inhabitants, if anyone sends us a message, then that being is acting as a channel or medium.

Many times, there are many deep experiences in meditation. Our senior masters are also having it. If we are not able to decode those messages, we will not be able to understand them.

To explain this more clearly, I would like to give you the message of the program of meditation-festival on the birthday of Mahavatar Babaji on 30 November 2023. To celebrate his birthday, we all were talking about the life of Babaji. All of a sudden, a strange kind of process of change started and transformation began. We all were meditating together and I started feeling Babaji's presence. The meditation process had started with the chants of Shivaay.

I was feeling Kundalini Shakti rising up and descending along with Shiva, Shaktis and all other powers. The chanting was clear, sh…shiv…shivay! Energies were risen up above the crown chakra. Shivay! Om Namah Shivay!

In the same way, it was repeating again and again in a descending manner. In this way, a lot of divine energies were felt in the presence of Mahavatar Babaji and the entire process was completed. All the work was being completed in the presence of Babaji.

The energy of all the meditators was rising. It was an ascension. At the time of this ascension, many people were seeing light, peace, shine, rainbow colors, etc. Everyone's energy was getting ready for further ascent.

At that time, the energy of the heart chakra rose in a circular shape and moved forward. Many people were meditating together. In such a situation, everybody's energy was coming together and connecting with everyone's hearts and becoming one.

In the consciousness of the collective energy, that energy was moving upward at a very high speed and in that increasing energy was forming a circumference or circle of energy. The presence of many consciousnesses started being felt. All these experiences were happening to all the meditator brothers and sisters (Soul Brothers and Sisters) as per the awareness of their consciousness. But my consciousness got connected with that supreme consciousness, got completely connected and became very deep and dense. Feeling such a ascension, it seemed that for any ascent we do not have to ever leave the world, go anywhere or go from one dimension to another.

I had touched the hand of my higher self, through the energy of my Earth in the presence of Babaji. It felt as if a very large part of me had merged with him and became one, or a small part of him had come into me. There is only one thing happening. We are a part of God's higher consciousness and when we go into His true essence, only His energy remains. The energy that was there was very powerful, very deep.

When my consciousness was rising to such a high level, all those who were sitting in the group or the energy created by everyone, were in a state of influence of that energy in the presence of Babaji. Something happened that no one could understand. To know that something is happening, when anyone ascends, there is a change in energy. Some energy goes into DNA, some gets absorbed into the environment, some energy goes into natural elements. But after such an experience, there is a great change in life.

Such tasks start happening which are meant only for Babaji's disciples. Whatever process Babaji is talking about in this changing era, it is the process of Ascension only. *"Merge yourself with those five great spirits"*, Babaji says, this ascension experience that some people can have with earthly life, in some moments, in some days or in some years, depends on each person's own desire or his capacity. Many people ascended with me that day.

Many of my soul sisters experienced their souls and many must have known themselves in the form of a soul. Ascension means reaching the next shift while remaining in the same body in which we were born or in which we came from our parents. Even after Ascension, we are still living here on Earth.

Even after achieving Ascension, for which we came here on earth to achieve, we are not leaving the body. Ascension is to connect with our divinity while still in a body and to connect with new energies while still in the body, to talk to them, to be transformed, to give up our old energies and to connect with new energies.

The night of 30 November 2023 was a very important night. Though we came back from that situation but Babaji's presence remained for many hours. Babaji answered many questions. Babaji was asking me to come to the cave. I said Babaji, we will make the program for next year. But it seemed as if Babaji's energy was pulling me and telling me to come into the cave now, come into the cave now. A very loud *"Shoonay"* came and took me into one of its grids or circles in such a way that I was sitting inside the cave. The vibrational field of those caves was such strong that it took me straight from the room to the cave. Along with Mahavatar Babaji, Lahari Mahasaya Ji and Sri Sri Yukteswar Giri Ji were also present in the cave. Seeing me, Sri Sri Yukteswar Giri ji said, *"Yogu! You are being given a task. You have to teach the people of the earth."*

I asked, *"What kind of teaching, what are you saying, Gurudev?"* Babaji was sitting in front of me. He said,

"There are many old energies which are sitting in deep inside the people, those energies have to be released and you have to tell that process to the people."

I wanted to know from him what was being talked about. Are they earth bound spirits who are sitting around the earth? Are they old energies which are not able to leave the earth, which are sitting stuck in the earth, inside the earth, in the sky, on plants, on trees or at other places. Is there need of bidding farewell to these energies?

I asked again, *"what kind of energy is this and where are these?"* Gurudev said, *"These are the energies which are present within every person. They are present inside each person's body. These are the energies that a person takes from outside. These are the energies which are present in this body. And it sticks to different places inside this body and it starts consuming the energies of that person, sucking them in. These are the energies that the person has collected from different places, different environments, situations, people, reasons, times, times ages that have stuck with them. You have to show a person how to separate themselves from these old energies and these are not only present in the environment as an earth bound soul but also in the individual."*

Lahari Mahasaya Ji was smiling. While smiling, the light was getting deeper around him and he was smiling softly. Mahavatar Babaji smiled at me as if everything will be done. It seemed as if he himself would get it done. I didn't think about anything else and I agreed. "This work is very big", I said,

"Who will tell the procedure, Gurudev? Which method will work here?" Mahavatar Babaji told me how to work. I said, *"Who will come and how the work will be done?"* He said, *"Only you prepare yourself for this role. Only those whom I have selected will be present. They will come and do the same. You just have to show them the methods so that they can work on themselves and start working in that place and in those countries."*

Mahavatar Babaji said that you should never forget that you should always keep the energy of Hanuman Ji with you. Hanuman Ji's energy is doing a lot of work on the earth at this time. For your safety, you always have to keep the energy of Hanuman Ji with you.

I was feeling very confused within. I came out of the cave. As soon as I opened my eyes,

I told everything to Gupta Ji. Gupta Ji told me to go back to the cave again and get answers for some questions. I again reached the cave this time through my consciousness. Babaji, Yukteshwar Giri Ji, Lahari Mahasaya Ji were still sitting in the cave. I asked Babaji the same questions that Gupta Ji told me to ask. Babaji answered some questions, told me what this work was and, in this way, gave me guidance.

We realize our true self and deep connection with our Inner God – Goddess. The basic key is to say it again and again, to let people know about the grandness within them. Suppose if we think of a great tree and how it was first a seed only. You may think about the capacity of the seed to grow into a huge tree, living for so many years. The other seed also had a capacity to not grow and to die in few years.

Thank you Babaji!

16 VASUDEV KUTUMBAKAM

I cannot express in words the kind of feelings and energy that starts flowing in my heart again and again for Mahavatar Babaji. He is a loving father who gives his love to mankind. Mahavatar Babaji is not only an extraordinary Brahman living being but He is present in the form of consciousness in the entire universe or the worldly and transcendental worlds. Here I seemed to be having such an experience of Babaji which was inspiring me again and again to give a message to the world. It was the night of 30 December 2020. Babaji came in front of me and started giving the message in his voice, for the work which needs to be started from 1st January 2021.

Babaji wanted to start my own online program to give the message of peace to the whole world, this message of Babaji was so profound that the same message was repeated again and again that the world peace program has to be started from 1st January. I wondered how I would be able to do all this in one day, bringing in speakers, making a list of topics, etc. I was in a state of confusion. But Babaji helped me to finalise the names and topics from our previous experiences.

He used to give me consent in sign language. Where there was no consent, my body communicated it in a different way. I started creating different titles for the term *"Global Peace and Vegetarian"*. But I was a little worried as I had to start within one day. I was wondering, *"What is so special about a first date?"*

The words *"Vasudev Kutumbakam"* came to me on the day of 1st January. I was even more surprised when I saw on Google that January 1 has actually been declared as *"Global Family Day"*. Now the question was how to take the help of mass communication to convey the message about this new program to the people.

Through Babaji's guidance, many topics were written in my conscious mind through my subconscious mind at that time. Now the question was who will do this work and how, how will it be manifested, Babaji told me in a very beautiful way. Babaji said that whoever will come, whoever will speak will be those people whose birthday is on the same day. I was very surprised as it was quite an interesting thing and Babaji gave his message for the entire 31 days that is from 1st to 31st of January month. I got my Masters and through them all the messages of non-violence, love, truth, solidarity, harmony, goodwill, respect for others, vegetarianism and meditation were spread. Time and again Babaji himself revealed the secrets of the work he chose to do to raise the consciousness of the earth and also followed them himself. He himself suggested a way to eliminate them. Babaji guided me with such a self possessing powers of Brahma, Vishnu and Mahesh in my entire life.

Babaji guided me in different ways, sometimes secretly, in meditation, sometimes in front, in different forms, that is, Babaji gave me messages and showed me paths. My soul became so happy after receiving His kindness, love and knowledge that sometimes it is said that whenever God is happy, the Guru is also happy at that time.

Babaji was very happy. There was a smile on Babaji's face and I was always considering myself lucky. Our program *"Vasudev Kutumbakam Global Peace and Vegetarian"* started online from 1 January 2021 and was completely successful. Global Peace online meditation is still ongoing under different names. In 2021, it ran five times a day.

If humans can shift their patterns of thinking, more and more people will awaken. Babaji believe that there is something higher and they worked towards it. These masters are just showing an example of what we can do.

Om Tatsat!!

Thank you Babaji!

17 SERVICE IS LAW OF NATURE

Once, when Mahavatar Babaji told me that why on earth it always happens that everyone wants to know the soul, also wants to know the truth, but everyone ignores the one through which it is known. So I asked Babaji a question, *"Babaji, what do you want to tell through this?"* So Babaji showed me his posture and started explaining to me and said, *"Look, everyone ignores their body. It is a different matter that Mahatma Buddha had also ignored the body and such people who do penance, fasting, burn and melt their body through penance."*

Babaji made it very clear through this that the body is the medium through which you are able to know all this, hence, why do you ignore the body. If we want to gain knowledge, and want to know the truth then we cannot achieve anything without our body. Nothing can be found or known at the cost of the body. Therefore, the importance of truth was told that we have to value our body and also the family in which we live, the people who are with us, we have to take as much care of them as we take care of our body.

Babaji gave messages about purification through the experience of cleaning the leaves. On one hand, he was talking about purification and at the same time, he was giving the message of service. The mind is situated between the body, intellect and ego and it needs the purification.

This meant that there was a message of purification of the mind by cleaning the trees, cleaning the leaves and cleaning the surroundings of that place. Like Babaji was saying that the mind becomes pure only by giving because the mind has a great impact on all the other four levels of the human being. That is why Mahavatar Babaji asked humans to give selflessly.

Babaji serves only for the welfare of the people, for the welfare of the disciples, for the welfare of the individuals, for good personality, health, prosperity, freedom from the bondage of karma and to attain that truth, that love, that divine love. Babaji was giving the message for energy transformation on earth, divine love, compassion and freedom from karmic bondage which are very important to move into the fifth and higher dimension.

Whatever Babaji was saying about serving, to some extent he was speaking for the person's own welfare. This will benefit the individual and every living being. That is, only by doing good and serving selflessly, a person's conduct and nature can become pure like a saint.

Such a saint, free from the bondage of karma, engages in continuous service. If people have love for God, they start understanding that God is within everyone. So, he cannot live without giving because it is given out of love from him.

Now either that person first understands himself or he understands that there is God within every person and if he starts serving without any discrimination, then along with his karmic bondages, his old bonds will also be broken. It can be purified very quickly.

Babaji's message here was for service. Attention is necessary to serve. That is why attention is needed. Mahavatar Babaji himself has emphasised service along with meditation. Service teaches us to bow down. Destroys our ego. Seva frees us from our karma. Babaji gave this message of exchange of service.

I also wanted to share a message here because by serving, a person becomes free from ego. Most of the time during 2013-14, when this message was being given, there were such energies that people were doing service, moving forward in spirituality, meditating, taking knowledge but, if ego remains in them then the person will not be fully purified. That is why so much emphasis was laid on service, to give to society.

Somewhere Babaji wanted to tell me that now if you want to come to me then you should become prosperous and prosperity is achieved through service. It is also said in the Bible that it is easier for camel to go through the eye of a needle but he who has the value of money in his mind cannot enter the abode of God.

Giving always increases by serving. We have to become the ones who share the energies that are coming to the earth at this time. Service is important because to give is to receive. When we give to someone, we also receive something and every person has to give and take something to make himself complete. So, he must fully enter into service, and until then he is not even considered complete.

So, here Babaji has explained the need for service. Service is the law of nature. We have to understand through our thoughts that there is a law of exchange in nature. We have already taken from nature, so now we must give back to it as well.

Imagine if we had to purchase oxygen, how much money would we have to pay? We already pay for water, yet nature provides us with so many resources in an uninterrupted way.

Earth is a serving society. It is continuously giving and if there is no balance in the exchange, then there will be pain and sorrow. By not adopting the law of exchange, the energies with which the Earth is moving towards higher dimensions, and higher vibrations, will be disrupted.

Hence, it is the duty of each consciousness to maintain the balance. And Babaji wanted us to understand the meaning of balance.

Nature is giving us. Babaji explains that you come here to the caves and you like this silence here, my presence is being felt near the cave because you are getting the peaceful environment here. You have come this far to do penance. You find peace here. You feel me here with peace, feel me, feel my presence and feel good because of nature, the atmosphere, the winds and, the coolness. Here, there is silence, a presence of peace, and emptiness that brings us joy. But what are we giving in return for this?

We try to give everything to our children, being selfish. There is no prohibition in giving, but whatever we are taking from nature; we also have to pay back. Be quiet for sometime. Do Meditation.

Thank you Babaji!

Grow Hope
Save Nature
30 MAR 2024

18 SHRI NARENDRA MODI IS YOUR GURU BHAI

In July 2013 when Gupta Ji and I were traveling by train. That night, while meditating, I fell asleep. It is said that when we fall asleep while meditating at night, our sleep transforms into Yoga Nidra because our consciousness remains engaged in meditation. At that time, in those vibrations we enter a deep meditative state. This is something that Brahmarishi Patriji used to teach us.

That night, I heard Babaji's voice. He gave me a message, *"The sun is about to rise. The sun is about to rise from the west."*

At that moment, I became aware and I saw the sun in my vision. I wanted to understand its meaning. We all know that the sun rises in the east, not the west. Then, I realized the deeper meaning of this message. The sun represents light, knowledge, and awakening. Any consciousness that brings light to the world is like the rising sun. Babaji was telling me that a great awakening was coming from the west.

I fully understood this message when Narendra Modi Ji was elected as the Prime Minister of India. His divine work, his vision for the world's consciousness, progress, and development, and his dedication to Indian culture and the well-being of all people, it all became clear to me. Mahavatar Babaji had been pointing me toward Narendra Modi Ji.

Then, in early 2024, Babaji gave me another message. *"You will call Narendra Modi Ji your Guru Bhai."* I was surprised. Narendra Modi Ji, my Guru Bhai? Babaji confirmed it again: *"Yes, he is your Guru Bhai. I am his Guru too. And whenever you meet him, you must address him in this way."* I felt incredibly blessed.

At first, I struggled to understand how to accept this. But Babaji continued to guide me. He reminded me of something significant, an incident from 2020. On December 30, 2019, Babaji told me, *"You must start meditating for the peace and harmony of the Earth. This is very important. You have to do it."* And I had to start on January 1, 2020. I wondered, what is special about this day? That's when I learned that January 1st is World Family Day.

While designing the poster for this meditation initiative, I said, *"Babaji, we will definitely do this for world peace."* As I was creating the poster, a phrase kept coming to my mind—*"Vasudhaiva Kutumbakam"* (The world is one family).

I wrote *"Vasudhaiva Kutumbakam"* on the poster.

Later, when India hosted the G20 Summit, and world leaders gathered in India, I saw the same words everywhere. Across the roads, walls, banners, and posters in Delhi, the phrase *"Vasudhaiva Kutumbakam"* was written.

It was Prime Minister Narendra Modi Ji's message to the world—a reminder that we are all part of one global family.

At that moment, I felt a deep realization. I saw clear evidence in this material world that there is a shared consciousness between us, and that consciousness is Mahavatar Babaji.

Thank you Babaji!

19 OUR CONSCIOUSNESS DETERMINES WHAT WE REALLY ARE

When it was the time of Covid pandemic, I wanted to know what kind of experience was happening on earth. I asked this question many times in meditation, what is this? What world is this going on in? What is going on in this world, so I was getting instructions from somewhere that this is a kind of transition period, where we are on a journey. Then at night in a dream state I was shown a scene that the entire earth was moving from the third dimension to the fifth dimension. This happened when Babaji told me about setting up the memorial.

It was shown to me that there is a very big earthly empire and we are going from the middle to the fifth dimension. In the fifth dimension, everyone around was working for spirituality because they were all locked in their houses. In the fourth dimension there is spirituality and love everywhere. They showed how we can talk to the elements, our angels, our spirit guides. We can establish communication with them. And all this work was being done by me online on the Pyramid Light Facebook page. I was teaching people there how we can establish communication with that kingdom, how we can send our love to our loved ones through telepathy and I was chosen to teach this.

Here was the message of Babaji, who was showing from time to time what we were going through. In the fourth dimension we saw that we are crossing it and there are many people in this world who not only have capabilities, but also formal capabilities.

They can also heal others but they are not able to achieve those extraordinary abilities without tuning into their inner systems. We are nearing the Ascension and taking a clear sense of responsibilities for our consciousness. At this time Babaji also told me to connect with various animal deities. Babaji showed me that people are not aware of their divine abilities.

He told, *"I have come to you to make you understand and tell you that there are many such abilities within you that you should know about."*

He further said, *"Every dimension has some rules and principles which are very important for the vibration of that dimension. The vibration of each dimension is of a higher rate than the one before and as we move into each higher dimension the reality becomes more clear and detailed. There is a greater form of knowledge in it and we become more free, more powerful, and have more opportunities to create reality."*

When I got a chance to establish contact, then not only animals came there but nature and all the five elements also connected with me. Somewhere in it, spirits also came, allowing us to talk with those who are dead and no longer in this world. We can also talk to them because so much light had gathered that it was clearly visible.

Here it seemed that the suffocation that we felt in the dimensions below – in the third dimension – felt as if we were in a class in a school. But now it seemed as if state of consciousness had spread. It was like a kind of third dimensional operating system which was very limited and was bound by rules, now it is no longer limited. I was experiencing the emergence of the divine gifts.

We were taught that we are solid, that we cannot meet, that there are walls between us. We are different, there are differences among us. We work on the principle of gravity. Things can never end. We cannot read people's minds. Who knows what is going on in each person's mind. But gradually we were told that we were not subservient. We are witnessing people being healed quickly and more frequently. Energies are shifting. Our bodies are multidimensional.

This was a huge change. This experiment happened repeatedly with me where my things were made to disappear again and again and then after some time, they would automatically come back in front the same place. Babaji gave me such experiences through communication and told me that you can read the minds of others and can also convey the emotions of your mind to others. I felt ascended and also felt supernatural powers in positive ways.

All this stuff was given to me in 2020. If we look back at things today, how those things were shown from time to time. That entire fourth dimension was very clear and obvious. The fourth dimension is a kind of bridge which connects the third and fifth dimensions. Some people will say that we are at the end of the fourth dimension and some will say that we have entered the fifth dimension. Both things are correct. By the end of 2020, we had entered the fifth dimension.

Now we are realising our insight and awakening. We are feeling clean and calm from within. We feel that our emotions are changing. Babaji showed all these things from time to time and he told that here in the third dimension there is only time but in the fourth dimension as it is now it is converting into liquidity and that knowledge is coming. Our subtle form, our subtle powers can be changed. A holy person who is clean can have the ability to make changes through his subtle body. It was a very important and beautiful experience with Mahavtar Babaji.

Thank you Babaji!

20 DIVINE ENERGY OF LOVE

Love is a kind of natural force which is much greater than the mind. As soon as it comes in contact with any person, it starts casting a spell and it becomes beyond knowledge and understanding.

When Mahavatar Babaji invited us to stay for a few days at that place near his cave, he spread a divine energy of love. The energy of love is sometimes in the form of the hum of whirlpools, sometimes with the fragrance of flowers, sometimes with the wonderful flow of natural scenes, sometimes in the form of clouds and winds flying over the mountain peaks, sometimes in different ways like this. It seemed as if that divine energy, that divine love of Babaji was reaching you.

Babaji said, *"I am everywhere and this is love. Love is the power that has the ability to change everything. Love is the only solution to war. There is only one solution to all the problems of the world – love. Therefore, spread the energy of love in everything. This is a prayer that has to be offered for the peace of the entire world, for world peace and for harmony."*

Prayer is the only way to move any energy from point A to prayer point B, to any person, place or any situation that needs that prayer. Through the power of love the prayer energy is carried safely to its destination.

If we intend or speak the most important change for the Golden Earth, then I can give that energy through my life energy, through my power. In this way the energy of love acts as a carrier. Suppose you love me, then those feelings of yours will be transmitted to me through love. Love in itself is a sacred energy and it is also the biggest healer.

Do you know what the disease is? The meaning of disease is disharmony. This means there is no harmony. There is a disharmony and we can transform the disharmony through the introduction of harmony. This means only love is the greatest harmoniser of the solar system. It is active practical metaphysical energy.

Love is not only theoretical or abstract. Neither it is only a feeling but it is beyond. When a person begins to realise his true position in the Cosmos, why am I here? He must have begun to manifest his great power. Love is the greatest power. Love is not the result of ignorance but it is the result or outcome of self awakening. This is a direct result. Therefore, mankind must become enlightened to be able to harness the powerful energy called love. It is a powerful energy used by Jesus, Buddha and Patanjali and many other incarnations because they were using only love energies. They were enlightened beings. They were beings who believed in state of mind. They considered love, not just an emotion but state of mind. All pervasive energy, which they could feel when they had awareness, and developed the right state.

The right state of awareness means a state of spontaneity where they have reached and they broadcast outward again in a very practical way to all people to understand what we are doing. What are you doing, what you have to do, you have to understand. After enlightenment or after gaining knowledge, if we look at the results of what Jesus did. He used it as carrier waves using his immense magnetic powers and as a result, he could revive the dead and enable the lame to walk.

What we can see in the love of Sai Babaji is we can feel that impossible is possible. So, we can also co-create, if we use our potent forces correctly. I was just feeling that Babaji was saying that *"I am always everywhere. It's great that you have come here to my cave. But*

I am not limited, present in the cave only. My presence is everywhere, only you have to resonate with it."

It was happening in the air, in the silence and actually it is all happening in each cell of element. There is only love, love and love and this is why we are feeling so happy and so peaceful because we are now totally in harmony. So, the message Babaji was conveying was without any words and appearances.

He has said everything that humanity needs today. Babaji conveys these messages to mankind without even saying a few words. He didn't even speak and everything was done. This is that love, this is that energy. When humanity awakens, it starts understanding the feelings of others and the problems of others. Then that love will become alive, it will become vibrant and it will spread everywhere. The more love he gives, the more love will spread in the air. But love is neither a right nor a status.

Every human being should have love and start loving the world and start loving equally without limits. Babaji explained a beautiful meaning of love *"Love, which has no limits, it is infinite like the sky. May such love become your nature, let it become infinite, let it become equal for everyone, let it go away from limitedness for everyone, let it become limitless from limitedness, let it become infinite."* When the chakra of love opens in our heart chakra, then the entire creation will become love and start radiating the energy of love at a very high speed.

I was feeling as if Babaji was giving the same message, saying the same thing that when a child is familiar with the energy of love, when the entire nature is familiar with the energy of this love, then why not human beings become familiar with the energy of love?

Why doesn't he wake up from that world of attachment? Why doesn't he wake up from that world where there is only selfishness? There is selfishness of man against man, of country against country, and of each one against another. Why doesn't he wake up and recognise that love is unconditional and without any selfishness?

Babaji says, *"The love that you expect me to give, you should recognize and know that this love is also in your heart. Pure Love is not mere attachment; with it goes beyond mere attachment."* As soon as we will know this, our energy will ascend. Our heart chakra expands and creates such a divinity at that place that we will become self-awakened.

Thank you Babaji!

21 BLISSFUL MOMENTS WITH MAHAVATAR BABAJI

When we made the program to go to Babaji's Cave, then Covid came, and we had to change our program within 10 days. However, everything became fine again. So, we planned the program once more with our soul sisters and soul brothers. Babaji gave me some indications.

As Babaji always used to tell us, we had to come, and we had to make some preparations. He also told us that some souls would join from Kolkata, and it happened exactly as he said.

When our program was set, and we were preparing to go there, Babaji gave me a message: "This time, I will meet you physically there." I was overjoyed at the thought of finally meeting Babaji in person. He made all the necessary preparations, and then the day arrived in April when we had to go to Babaji's Cave.

With a new hope in our hearts, we set out on our journey, eager to meet Babaji. We arranged our schedule and embarked on our journey. The day finally came when we arrived in Dunagiri. As we prepared to go to Cave, we traveled through various places in Uttarakhand, getting closer to our destination.

Upon reaching there, I did not receive any indication that I would meet Babaji. I couldn't see him in front of me, nor did I feel his presence. We didn't meet Babaji at that time. We started our trekking, climbing the paths towards our destination. Suddenly, we reached a familiar spot, the same place where the Yogoda Satsang Society is located. If you have been to that mountain, you must have seen this breathtaking view. An open sky, some rocks, and a peaceful, beautiful landscape leading towards Babaji's cave.

When I reached there, a deep question arose in my mind: *"Babaji, I haven't seen you yet. Where will I meet you? When will I meet you?"* A sense of curiosity filled my heart. But I did not receive any indication. My eyes reflected a subtle sense of disappointment, not complete sadness, but a longing unfulfilled. I asked Babaji, *"When will I meet you, Babaji? Your cave is about to come."* I thought I would meet him on the way, but I didn't.

As I closed my eyes for a few moments and sat in silence, suddenly, I felt something. Babaji and

Yukteshwar Giri ji both appeared before me. They sat there, almost as if they were in a flying chariot. Babaji sat beside me, and told me that we needed to create a place. He always emphasized that we had to make a place. For that, we needed to find the right land. For many years, I had been trying to find such a place, a piece of land where we could establish something meaningful.

I had been searching for this land tirelessly. Although there were some pyramids in Haldwani, still, when Babaji sat me in that flying chariot, he gave me a sign. Babaji started showing me something. In the foothills of Babaji's cave, the land below had been chosen. It was as if the place had been decided. I understood Babaji's sign and felt that he was pointing to the land that would be chosen for our meditators. We would build an ashram in the name of Mahavatar Babaji.

On the other hand, I was also feeling that I had been praying to Babaji for many days. I had a desire that I wanted to create a valley, a sacred space for Mahavatar Babaji. But I knew I could not do it alone. I needed a team, people who would work and stay there. However, I had not found the right people yet.

Babaji and Yukteshwar Giri kept me within that radius, and I enjoyed this experience. It felt like the time had come. Things were falling into place. Some decisions had been made. After that, I got up and started walking towards Babaji's cave.

As we reached Babaji's cave, I sat down inside. The moment I sat there, I felt a strange restlessness in my body. I was unable to sit comfortably, shifting from one place to another. My eyes suddenly fell on a person sitting inside the pyramid, staring straight ahead. But I did not pay much attention to him and tried to focus on meditation. In this way, I also felt that in Babaji's cave, the place that initially seemed uncomfortable to me, finally became a suitable place to sit, and I settled into my meditation. While meditating, the same thought kept coming to my mind that Babaji had said, *"I will come in physical form."* So, I wondered, when will Babaji appear? I was sitting in the cave, waiting.

Suddenly, a doubt arose in my mind. A little distance away, Gupta ji was sitting, watching me. He gestured towards the saint seated in the middle of the cave and indicated, *"He is Mahavatar Babaji."* I hesitated and thought to myself, no, this must just be his imagination.

It can't be true. I dismissed his words and did not pay much attention. But as I continued meditating, my eyes opened, and I noticed that the saint in the center of the cave was sitting in a unique mudra. A thought arose in my mind, Is this Babaji? I began conversing with him in my thoughts, but he remained still, his gaze fixed in one direction. He did not look at me even once. The cave was full, with about 15 to 20 people, our soul brothers and sisters, all in deep meditation. This process went on for a long time, yet one question kept repeating in my mind, Is this Babaji?

After some time, I began feeling restless, very restless. I gestured for everyone to leave, realizing they had been meditating for over an hour. As they quietly made their way out, I turned towards the saint, now with full devotion in my heart. With folded hands, I prayed, Babaji, if you are truly the one, please give me a sign. If you are the one, please give me a smile. By then, the cave was empty. Everyone had left. There was no one inside except the saint.

In front of him lay a box of sweets and a single rose. I was trying to recall everything. My heart was pounding so fast that I could hardly bear it. Maybe, he is Babaji. Maybe he had been waiting for the right moment to reveal his presence to me. It felt as if he himself had guided me to send everyone out of the cave.

And when everyone had truly left, he gestured for me to take the rose and the prasadam from the box of sweets. But I was stubborn. I insisted, "*If you are Babaji, then I want you to give me the prasadam yourself*". At that moment, my heart felt as if Babaji was fulfilling my request. With his own hands, he picked up a piece of sweet from the box. A slight smile appeared on his face.

My consciousness understood. This is Babaji. Tears welled up in my eyes as I bowed in deep reverence. You promised to give me darshan, and you came. I spent a long time in his presence, soaking in the peace and divine energy surrounding me. When I finally stepped out of the cave, I paid my respects once again. I sat outside the cave for a long time.

Later, as I walked back, I shared my experience with a few soul brothers and sisters. I had already confided in a few people that Babaji would give darshan this time. Even Gupta ji had told me, He is Babaji. He was curious, he asked around about the saint who had appeared in the cave. Someone replied, we have never seen him before. He just appeared a day or two ago. We don't know where he came from.

That night, back at our camp, as we sat around the fire, I felt something stirring deep within the earth like subtle vibrations, distant drumbeats, an unexplainable melody. It felt as if something was being revealed, as if something was connecting to a higher realm.

Thank you Babaji!

22 CRYSTALS ENERGIES TO RAISE YOUR CONSCIOUSNESS

In 2022, I received a message from Mahavatar Babaji about Crystals. I was surprised that Babaji was talking about crystals. However, I had loved crystals since my childhood. I liked its colours, structures and its different jewelry. Babaji told me to spread wisdom about crystal energy to my soul brothers and sisters. The first thought that came to my mind was that do I have to start a business because whatever service I have done for Planet Earth and Humanity has always been free of cost. So, I was unable to understand, Then I requested Babaji to explain me about it.

So, Babaji told me that humanity still has much work to do. There are some special specific crystals that can be used to support raising all human vibrations. It will be helpful to activate others extra levels of DNA. Many spiritual practitioners believe they are progressing through meditations and self-discipline, but that alone is not sufficient. There are some more deeper layers to work. Crystal energies are essential for higher spiritual evolution, and they must be understood and utilized.

I did not have much knowledge about crystals, so the question arose in my mind: who would teach me about them? And if I suggested certain crystals to someone, would they actually be helpful? I requested Babaji, *"You alone must impart this knowledge about crystals into my body, system, and DNA, so that I may share it with others."*

Babaji helped me understand the true nature of crystals. He explained that they are formed deep within the Earth and serve as its DNA—a chemically impregnated blueprint for evolution. Crystals act as storehouses, preserving the history of Earth's transformation over thousands of years. These formations interact with human bodies in unique ways, absorbing, focusing, conserving, and emitting energy, particularly along electromagnetic wave bands.

Each crystal has a distinct geometrical structure, and its color and mineral composition influence its effect on the human body. Just as the human body is composed of minerals, crystals contain their own unique mineral combinations. For instance, calcite is found in the human brain and plays a crucial role in cognitive processes. Similarly, when used correctly, crystals can assist in activating different layers of consciousness and aid in spiritual ascension.

During the COVID-19 pandemic, humanity's immunity weakened significantly. In such times, crystals play a crucial role in restoring balance and enhancing well-being.

Babaji showed me visions of how crystals are required for light body activation. Activating this light body is essential for spiritual evolution, and crystal energy facilitates this process.

Regardless of whether a soul is mature or still evolving, everyone can benefit from the power of crystals. They work on all levels—physical, mental, emotional, and spiritual promoting holistic health. Babaji made me realize why understanding and utilizing crystals is important for ascension.

If the cells in our body are fully enriched with minerals, they generate light, allowing us to connect with higher realities. You can also consciously use crystals to activate them within your body. For example, if you want to work on your throat chakra, sacral chakra, or any other chakra, you will be able to do so naturally as you attune to the energy of the crystals.

Babaji was focusing on the Rose Quartz crystal and showed me a heart, indicating that planet Earth needs love energy.

The lack of love for oneself, for people, for the planet, for nature, and unconditional love is something we can address through this energy. Crystals act as an atomic accelerator, a kind of device to activate human energies. Babaji told me that these were used many times before, so why not use them now to raise our vibrations and elevate our consciousness?

Babaji explained how crystals can be used to activate chakras and bring transformation. I saw this happening firsthand. In 2023, the number 111 kept appearing to me, symbolizing a powerful portal energy. The *"111 soul sisters"* who used these crystals experienced transformation in their lives. We worked with Rose Quartz Towers and Rose Quartz Hearts, and I noticed symbolic drawings appearing almost like a language, revealing how portals were being created.

Babaji guided me in understanding how different crystals serve specific purposes. Whether it was pyrite, green aventurine, or lapis lazuli, each worked in a beautiful way. The crystals operated on a cellular level by clearing old patterns from the body, helping release dark energies and negative forces. In this black tourmaline is playing a key role in absorbing negative energies from places, people, or situations.

Since 2023, Babaji has reintroduced these crystal energies, although they have been used in ancient civilizations, such as by the Egyptians. Now, in this new age, these energies are being rediscovered and embraced once again.

I saw how these energies worked on everyone, so gentle, so loving, so full of compassion. Crystals can be used for anything. Whether it is lapis lazuli, malachite, moonstone, rhodonite, ruby, or turquoise, if we identify them correctly and activate them through proper programming, we can harness their full potential.

If used in the right direction and in the right way, these crystals can support us immensely. Babaji has naturally bestowed this knowledge upon me. He attuned my body to these energies, and now I am fully aligned with the crystal vibrations.

With this attunement, I can contribute to nature, planet Earth, and humanity by assisting in their ascension and fulfilling their spiritual needs.

Thank you Babaji!

23 AUSPICIOUS TIMES FOR EXPANDING HORIZONS

This experience, which I am going to share with you is from Varanasi. In 2023, we had planned to visit Kashi Vishwanath, and I felt a deep calling to visit the city of Shiva and also to complete my twelve Jyotirling journey. Another strong reason for this trip was my desire to meditate at the place where Lahiri Mahasaya Ji lived and where Mahavatar Babaji initiated Kriya Yoga to him and to the whole world.

As always, something guided me toward the right place. While searching for a hotel online, I kept feeling drawn to a particular one. When I finally booked it, I wasn't surprised to learn that it was near Lahiri Mahasaya ji's home. I knew I had to go there for meditation.

After reaching Varanasi, we took a boat ride on the Ganga in the evening. The next morning, I woke up at 5:30 AM and felt drawn to Dashashwamedh Ghat. As I walked towards it, I saw the crowd, people bathing in the holy river, boats floating, and the stairs filled with devotees. While walking there, it was 5:45 AM, and there were very high stairs. During those days, I had severe knee pain, which caused me a lot of discomfort.

I walked a few steps and as soon as I went down the stairs, my legs began to tremble, and a sharp pain took over my knees. I was unable to take another step. So, I sat down over there and closed my eyes, a tear fell from my eyes and I asked Mother Ganga, *"Even after coming to this city, will I not be able to come down to touch you?"*

I could not move a step ahead or a step back and Gupta ji was sleeping in the hotel, so I closed my eyes, and I prayed.

Within two minutes, something changed. My legs felt fine, as if an invisible force had healed me. I stood up, feeling strong again, and walked down effortlessly toward Mother Ganga. I saw everyone enjoying and taking a dip in the holy river, but I had just gotten up and come. I had not brought extra clothes with me, and this thought kept running through my mind as I walked around.

At that moment, a Woman standing near a boat called me. I didn't know her, but she smiled and asked me *"Are you feeling like taking a bath in Ganga ji?"*

A small smile came on my face and with a low voice I answered, *"Yes, but I do not have any clothes."*

She said, *"You come, clothes will dry up."*

There was something unusual about her presence, something divine. Without thinking much, I stepped into the Ganga, the lady holds my hand and I started taking a bath. I took a bath for a long time. As I bathed, boats full of people passed by, but now when I remember, none came close to me as The Lady would push the boat backwards with her one hand. After some time, I stepped out of the river, and The Woman walked out too.

When I asked her where she was from, she said, *"Delhi."* I was surprised, what were the chances? I told her I was from Delhi too. I felt something different in her words. While, I was changing my clothes, I thought, maybe she will help me, but she had already left, I don't know who she was, but my consciousness was saying, as if, Babaji had come, but, even in thinking, this thought of mine, that, in my life, whatever is happening with me, Babaji does it, Lord Shiva does it but before I could ask more, she had disappeared.

Something deep inside me knew, this was Babaji's presence. Whether in physical form or through an experience, he always finds a way to guide me.

☆☆☆

As I was leaving the Ghat, I saw a sign with the name *"Lalita Devi"* and felt a strong pull to visit her temple. I had thought that I will visit Kashi Vishwanath

Temple with Gupta ji, So let's visit the Devi temple now. But instead, without realizing it, my steps led me straight to Kashi Vishwanath instead of the Devi temple. I had planned to visit it later with Gupta Ji, So I was about to turn back and leave, but someone said *"Once you enter the temple, you don't turn back and leave."* I agreed and went, after receiving the darshan of Shivshakti, and then left the temple. I returned to the hotel and narrated the whole experience to Gupta ji.

My consciousness told me *"Babaji himself bathed me."* It is well known that Mahavatar Babaji is an incarnation of Lord Shiva. He appears among humans in different forms, and on that day, I felt his divine presence before me. I am sharing my experiences with you all as sincerely as I can. I have seen and felt his presence many times, but neither do I nor anyone else can provide concrete evidence of the experiences we go through.

I would like to share an important truth with you all. If we look at our body, every human being's physical body is linked with the Root Chakra, where the Kundalini Shakti remains asleep. Unless one realizes this truth through Prana Karma, Sadhana, and Devotion, this energy remains asleep. However, for a Yogi to attain complete realization, the Kundalini Shakti must awaken.

The soul is divine and blissful, like Lord Shiva, residing within the Vyoma Tattva, or the Vishuddha Chakra where Shiva Tattva lies in a deep and dormant state. This dormant state must be awakened. Through breath, it moves into the throat, and with the presence of air in the throat, it enters a dormant state. The air residing in the throat itself is Neelkanth.

The center of our five chakras is Shakti, which is present in all our chakras. But when the energy is awakened in the root chakra then this energy ascend towards Sushumna and as it rises, it energizes and liberates each chakra, dissolving ignorance and leading to liberation. At the Agya Chakra, the form of Shiv Shakti is present. That is the union of nature and a human.

In the Bhagavad Gita, the Karma Yogi is described as the Kriya Yogi. Through meditation, people believe that establishing the idols of deities in the Agya Chakra helps them attain self realization. Meditation has been described in different ways, but if we are not experiencing inner peace during meditation, we must understand that we are not practicing it correctly.

There are three types of Nadis in the body - Ida Nadi, Sushumna Nadi, and Pingala Nadi. These three channels exist within us, and our life force energy influences the mind, often making it restless.

However, when the life force energy becomes steady, and the mind unites with it, one experiences divine realization.

Later that day, we went to Satyam Lok which is Lahari Mahasaya ji's asharam, where his samadhi is also present. We sat in meditation. I was experiencing a zero state. In the state of liberation, all truths become clear. When Ida and Pingala Nadis are balanced, restlessness disappears, and the Sushumna Nadi becomes active.

To share my experience, I must first lay the foundation. A Yogi must recognize three essential granthis in the body, Jiva Granthi, Hriday Granthi and Muladhara Granthi. These are also known as Brahma Granthi , Vishnu Granthi and Mahesh Granthi. A Yogi who transcends these three granthis is known as Tribhanga Murari. Through Omkar Kriya, when one unties the Hriday Granthi, all doubts are dissolved. With deep self-realization, an enlightened master becomes completely immersed, dissolving all accumulated impressions. In this state, he perceives Atmanarayan within himself, witnessing the divine presence of Narayan. In that moment, neither bondage nor liberation exist.

To understand this deeply, we must look at Kuthastha, the point between the eyebrows (the third eye). This is where Supreme Being and Soul reside. The Supreme Consciousness is pure knowledge and the source of all light. The Soul's Sun shines from this center. Without this presence, there would be no illumination.

When the mind enters the cave of spiritual consciousness, all suffering dissolves. In this state, the mind is neither distracted nor restless, it becomes completely still. As the breath stabilizes, the mind merges into the Kuthastha, aligning with the third eye, leading to the state of Divine Consciousness. This state, where the point of the third eye is illuminated, signifies that the inner light has awakened. It means that the breath is now flowing inward, moving through the Sushumna Nadi. In this state, it feels like the first light of dawn, subtle yet profound. After this, only a state of emptiness remains.

Now, I would like to share my experience. While meditating, I found myself immersed in shoonya (deep emptiness). There was a statue of Mahavatar Babaji in front of my meditation space. At that moment, I felt a strong inner instruction guiding me to sit in a different posture. I could clearly sense Babaji's presence. Following the guidance, I adjusted my posture accordingly.

After a while, Babaji instructed me to close my eyes and said, *"Meditate at the center of your breath. Be still. Detach from your senses. Focus. Meditate deeply in the center of your breath."*

As I followed his words, I saw Babaji behind me. He did a process on me. He has very long open hairs. He leaned towards me, He surrounded me from all sides, and Babaji cleared the further most delicate path for being one with Creator. Babaji removed even the slightest obstacle to further ascension. He himself initiated this sacred process within me. I felt as if I had reached the peak of my Pari nirvana state. I sensed that Babaji had activated certain layers of my DNA, which included specific mudras and symbols. I felt as if *"I am That."* I was feeling that I was getting evolved. I was able to understand the higher truth and the truth is always evolving and it is so vast. It was a process of evolution, where I was feeling that all my consciousness were combining. There was a tremendous shift that happened in my consciousness. It was as if a fine, hair-thin thread had been unlocked within my system, restructuring me at a deep level. I felt as though I had crossed the boundaries of ordinary existence and transformed into a more evolved being, not just multi-dimensional, but something beyond even that. It was an ascension, an expansion of consciousness.

Thank you Babaji!

24 KALKI DHAM INAUGURATION

I have always felt that the energy of Mahavatar Babaji and the energy of Shiva are the same. Do we see Shiva only as Shiva? No, we see Shiva as the supreme power, the only power in the universe, which we call Param Shiva, Paramatma, the formless divine presence. Yet, when this supreme power manifests in the visible world, Brahma creates, Vishnu sustains, and Shiva's great energy transforms and dissolves.

This realization came to me at least ten years ago. In my family, most of my brothers and sisters worshiped the Lord Kalki. They made idols, performed kirtans, and deeply revered Him. When I got married, I noticed the same devotion in my new family. But who is Kalki? According to Hindu belief, Kalki Avatar, is considered the 10th incarnation of Lord Vishnu. It is said that this divine incarnation will take birth when the era of Kalyug comes to an end.

Once, a relative of mine organized a kirtan and satsang in honor of the Lord Kalki, and we were invited. Around 250 to 300 people gathered. Since all the front seats were occupied, I went and sat on one of the chairs at the back. While, everyone was immersed in kirtan and bhajan, I sat in meditation. I felt an immense energy field forming, a vibration wheel of energy. Then, I heard a voice, *"In spiritual terms, you call this energy Mahavatar Babaji. The same energy is known to people as Kalki Avatar."*

I was stunned, speechless, and overwhelmed. I had seen images where Mahavatar Babaji, Lord Krishna, and even Jesus Christ was depicted together. This made me feel that these divine energies are interconnected. Just as Lord Krishna's energy manifested on Earth, Mahavatar Babaji's energy must have emerged at the same time. But this was my personal experience, a realization in meditation, and I trust my experiences completely because they have always revealed the ultimate truth to me.

Through my spiritual journey, I have always felt the presence of Shiva's power within the energies of Mahavatar Babaji—one power, the same power. Then, on February 18, 2024, I received news that the foundation stone for Kalki Dham in Sambhal district was going to be laid in the presence of highly respected saints, religious leaders, and the Honorable Prime Minister of India, Shri Narendra Modi Ji. As

I absorbed this information, I felt Babaji's energy guiding me. A voice within urged me to be present at that sacred moment, as the foundation of the new Earth was being laid. I have to sit in meditation, and offer my intensions onto that land along with the crystal energy.

However, attending the event seemed impossible. It was heavily secured, and entry required a pass that had to be obtained days in advance. I spoke to my family, who were also going, but they told me it was not possible, I needed an official pass. At that time, my younger sister, Kavita Gupta, had come to Delhi from Bhubaneswar. On the night of February 18, we were at our mother's house near the Delhi- UP border, and I felt an overwhelming restlessness inside. A strong inner calling told me, *'You have to go. You must be there. You have to sit at that place. This is the foundation stone of our new earth, and you have a role to play.'*

I surrendered to Babaji and said, *"I am ready to go, but I do not know how this will happen. If I am meant to be there for this sacred moment, then you must arrange everything."* I left the thought to the universe. Meanwhile, my sister, through her contacts in Odisha, tried to arrange passes, but there was no positive response. Midnight passed, then 1:00 AM, and still, there was no answer. Around 2:30 AM, we received a message that two passes had been arranged for us. It felt like divine intervention. By 3:00 AM, a car was arranged, and we immediately left for Sambhal.

Upon arrival, we presented our passes and were escorted to a special seating area, right in the heart of the gathering. From where I sat, I could see the helicopter landing, and moments later, I saw my Guru Bhai—Honorable Shri Narendra Modi Ji, stepping out. Alongside him were Yogi Ji, other revered saints, and distinguished guests. I was overwhelmed with emotions, covered in goosebumps. The moment was deeply significant.

As I listened to the speeches, I absorbed the messages with complete devotion. Just as Babaji had guided me, I meditated at the very spot where the foundation stone was laid, offering my intentions for Mother Earth, for the new earth being created. Along with me, several other awakened souls meditated, channeling energies for this divine transformation. After this deeply fulfilling experience, we met with saints and returned to Delhi.

Scriptures mention that Lord Kalki is described in the Agni Purana as a divine warrior riding a white horse named Devadatta, adorned with 64 mystical arts, and possessing miraculous powers granted by Lord Shiva. This signifies that the energy of Shiva is closely intertwined with the energy of Kalki. When we look at Mahavatar Babaji's work, we see that he has always chosen great saints and masters to reawaken divine knowledge throughout history. He guided Adi Shankaracharya in reviving Sanatan Dharma, he inspired saints like Kabir Das during times of spiritual decline, and he enlightened Lahiri Mahasaya to spread Kriya Yoga. Babaji has always ensured that the eternal wisdom reaches those who seek it.

Today, in this age, we do not need to renounce the world or wear saffron robes to attain spiritual awakening. Babaji's teachings remind us that we can connect with the divine in our daily lives. We can make our lives blissful through devotion, meditation, and the realization of our inner truth.

Thank you Babaji!

25 MESSAGE ABOUT RESURRECTION

I received Babaji's invitation to visit Caves this year. We planned our journey in 2024 to Babaji's caves with our 36 soul sisters and soul brothers. Our all arrangements were made, everything was set. but suddenly, I received a message from Babaji saying, *"you must stay in my foothills."* I had no idea where this place was or where I was meant to stay. I knew of only one place, which was at a distance.

Babaji kept giving me signs, again and again. When I searched on Google, I discovered a resort located exactly in his foothills, Vanprasth Resorts . Without hesitation, I called them and asked, *"I have to visit Babaji's cave and stay at your Resort."* The person replied, *"Our dates are already full. How will you find a place here?"* But I was certain. Babaji has given me a message. I have to come.

What happened next was remarkable. When they checked their bookings, the exact dates when we needed to stay were available. And so, our journey was set. We planned to go, just as Babaji had guided us.

Babaji had also revealed more to me about how he would come, when he would appear, and even the people who were chosen for this trip. He told me the precise moment when he would work on them, performing a process on their bodies.

And just as foretold, during our journey, everything unfolded in the same way.

☆☆☆

When we left for Mahavatar Babaji's cave, we also visited Haidakhan Babaji's Ashram. We went there to experience the divine energy of Haidakhan Babaji's place. So, there we were, making our way down, across the river, toward a cave. It was a truly beautiful experience during the journey.

As we were crossing the river, I suddenly noticed a few small shops along the way. One of them had a Rudraksha bead necklace. First and foremost, I completely surrender myself to Babaji, to Param Shiv, offering my life and everything I claim as mine. But at that very moment, I felt to buy the Rudraksha bead necklace to offer Shiva.

While everyone went to the temple, I chose to go to the cave and sit in meditation. The moment I closed my eyes, I saw Shiva standing in front of me.

He was very looking very happy. He gave me a sign to wear the necklace but I said to him, *"I picked it up with love and had brought this for you as an offering."* He smiled and said, *"This is my order. You must wear it."* I agreed and put it around my neck.

As I carefully observed, I felt the presence of Lord Shiva, the supreme himself consecrated the Rudraksha bead necklace. The moment I wore the Rudraksha bead over my heart, I experienced a profound sensation. Waves of energy radiated from my heart chakra, expanding outward. I could clearly perceive this with my inner vision. I silently expressed my gratitude and thanked him for this experience.

After wearing the Rudraksha, I sensed something new awakening within me. A fresh energy, a new heart chakra, was forming and spreading. I could see my spiritual ascension unfolding before my very eyes. I emerged from the cave with immense joy and a peaceful mind.

On our way back, I paid my respects to the temples. We descended to the Gautami River to take a bath, relishing the sacred waters. After some time, as we passed by the shops again, Gupta ji pointed at my neck and said, *"There's a reddish-orange hue all over it."* He then suggested that I should return the necklace. In that moment, I had completely forgotten what had happened in the cave just an hour ago. Without thinking, I gave the necklace back.

We crossed the river and continued our journey back. On the way, we stopped at a temple where a yagya was taking place. As I sat there in meditation, a vision of Lord Shiva appeared before me. He looked at me and reminded me, *"I had just given you that necklace, and you had worn it. Where is it now?* "I was stunned. What had I done? That necklace had been given to me by Shiva. A sudden realization struck me, and I ran back toward the shop. Desperately, I asked for the same necklace. But the shopkeeper had already gathered all his necklaces. I grew impatient. *"No, no, I need that exact necklace back!"*

In my forgetfulness, I had given away something precious, something that Lord Shiva himself had blessed me with. Even though all the necklaces looked the same, I yearned for the one I had received. The shopkeeper, sensing my urgency, carefully touched the threads of the necklaces, knowing that mine would be wet. He identified my necklace and handed it to me. *"Yes, this is yours,"* he said.

Lord Shiva's words echoed in my heart, *"Always wear this necklace. You will always be connected to me and to that supreme power."*

☆☆☆

I had a clear vision inside Babaji's cave where Mahavatar Babaji was there, along with Yukteswar Giri Ji. In that sacred moment, Babaji chose me to receive this initiation. He revealed to me the process by which a master's light body can transform into a human form.

He showed me how light energy, like a photon, can manifest into physical existence. In Kriya Yoga, there are many instances of this phenomenon that we read about, where Mahavatar Babaji first appeared as a radiant ball of light and gradually transformed into a human form.

Similarly, in Paramhansa Yogananda Ji's book, there is an account where a Master's light body appeared as a luminous sphere, which then transformed into a soft pink hue, revealing the form of Yukteshwar Giri Ji in the same form as his physical body.Swami Sri Yukteshwer Giri is an Indian monk,spiritual leader,yogi and guru of Paramahansa Yogananda and Swami Satyananda Giri.

If we talk about multi-dimensional personalities, it has been observed that in a state of celestial flight, this manifestation also occurs. A radiant sphere emerges from space, then transforms into a delicate pink blossom, within which Mahatma Buddha appears. These visions can be seen by the beings who are in a state of zero consciousness.

At such moments, Babaji and Yukteshwar Giri Ji, through higher consciousness, imparted the knowledge of this transformation, the transition from light to physical form and back into light, dissolving into space. He explained that photons, particularly bio-photons, play a crucial role in this process. Bio-photons, unlike ordinary photons, carry the essence of life. Babaji explained how cosmic atoms can create a new body even exactly the same as. When energy frequencies resonate at a higher level, they can influence molecular structures, triggering changes at a quantum level.

He revealed that just as molecules shift their quantum states and emit photons, the human body too can undergo transformation. The vibrational energy surrounding these photons can bring about changes in physical form. This process, where light descends into physical form and later ascends back into higher dimensions, was shared with me as sacred knowledge.

Babaji and Gurudev Yukteswar Giri Ji emphasized that what may seem extraordinary to us is simply a natural process for enlightened beings. They assured me that, in time, ascended souls too would be able to control our physical form, giving direct instructions to our bodies. This, they said, is the culmination of lifetimes of spiritual evolution, witnessing and participating in the ascension of Earth into higher dimensions.

Swami Yukteshwer Giriji told me, *"As I have been directed by God to serve on an Astral Planet as a savior,so you are also chosen. Now on planet earth you are helping souls for releasing karmas and attain liberation from rebirths. You are guided to release the people who are near death to transit in a smooth way."*

We stayed at the ashram and when we sat in meditation after the dinner on the night of the full moon, something incredible happened. Babaji came.

For some people, Babaji granted a complete experience. He worked on their Kundalini energy, activating their chakras. He attuned them through a divine process, using sound energy. It was a beautiful and sacred moment.

Earlier, I had promised Babaji to plant trees, fruit-bearing trees, to nourish the land and the people. And in perfect alignment, we found the opportunity. We planted 250-300 large trees, each about 4-5 feet tall like pomegranates, guava and other fruits of various seasons. We planted them in Vanprasth Ashram and also distributed saplings to local farmers in nearby villages. Meeting them, seeing their dedication to the land, and feeling their warmth touched our hearts deeply.

It was then that I realized—Babaji had shown me all of this in 2022. The foothills, the ashram, the trees, the people. He had already revealed it all to me, years before it came into being.

During our journey, Babaji gave us an urgent message, *"There is no more time to wait. Do your work, whatever you know, whatever you are skilled at. Do not chase liberation, awakening, or enlightenment. Just serve. Work for the welfare of humanity. Keep awakening others and keep moving forward. Do not stop. Just do your work."*

We were staying at Vanprasth Ashram, the place Babaji had told me about. I asked Alok ji about it. He had built the place and was a Kriya Yogi. He shared that he had initially chosen a different location, but through Babaji's inspiration and experiences, he decided on this particular place.

When I used to pray to Babaji, I would express my impatience and say, *"Babaji, I will not be able to take this place alone. Who will arrange it? Who will stay there? This is a big responsibility, and such work is not possible without soul brothers."* Alok ji told me that, he too had seen another place first, but he received a divine message to build the ashram here. And so, he did. I was overjoyed and told him, *"This is the same place that Babaji had shown me!"* And it had been built beautifully, a truly sacred space. Somewhere, on a deeper level, we are all one.

Thank you Babaji!

31/03/2024 06:29

26 ASCENSION TO THE FIFTH DIMENSION

The fifth dimension is the kind of dimension where we receive messages from God, where miracles happen every day, where our Holy Spirit is always ready to help us. After DNA activation, all your gifts become awakened. We realise that we live in a multi-dimensional world where there is never death. We are all multidimensional beings with the potential to transcend into higher dimensions and attain higher states of consciousness.

Our consciousness evolves with our own level of awareness according to our own state of mind. Many people are preparing and experiencing themselves to live in the fifth dimension. Many times our Holy Spirit is able to cure even serious diseases. His energy is being transferred even if we look at near death experiences or any other seemingly supernatural method such as awakening. This way of awakening our consciousness had an encounter with a part of the conscious light that was leading us into the matrix of the fifth dimension and at that time he had encounters with many Divine Masters such as Mother Mary, Jesus, Metatron and Angels etc.

We all have the ability to tap into our powers deep in the matrix of space. If we map the entire world or the entire grid of the world and take ourselves to the fifth dimension, we have many Guardian Angels and Guides who are ready at all times to help us in every situation and time.

If you are going through any serious illness, any supernatural power can appear in front of you and bring changes within you. From a spiritual point of view, the reality of the third dimension is one of technology, pain, suffering, illness, anger and greed. There is no spirituality in the third dimension. We can say that when these dimensions were created, they were not designed to last because there were these types of lower energies that were symbolised by fear, ego, greedy behaviour.

If we look at the fourth dimension beyond this, there is love, compassion and spirituality in it. You have angels and guides there to guide you. You may have contact with beings of higher dimensions and with the animal kingdom. In this book you can see that through the messages given by Babaji, we are crossing all those dimensions and moving forward towards the fifth dimension. The fifth dimension is a paranormal realm where miraculous healings occur. People there have extraordinary abilities. In the different levels of the fifth dimension we see that they have different experiences, they have different vibrations that beat at a higher vibration.

Many of us have had experiences in the fourth dimension over the years as we connect more with our angelic realm and spiritual inclinations. We are experiencing this dimension. When we have awakening experiences in insight we feel at peace within ourselves. Everything within us feels much lighter and less hard.

There is more liquidity in the fourth dimension, that is, there time, place, everything changes. In this way we are seeing the difference between our third dimension and fourth dimension. When we are in the fourth dimension we have clarity. We have the energy of gratitude. We live with these types of energies in the fifth dimension where we see everyone from a spiritual perspective and here we have no fear of time or space.

All types of mental and emotional fears are unable to enter the fifth dimension. There is no anger and fear, no hostility and no guilt. There you gain a lot of mastery over your thoughts, that is, your every thought is under your complete control. Whatever actions and events take place here, there are energies of love behind them because the energies of fear will not be able to remain there. If we experience fear in the fifth dimension we will immediately drop down to the fourth dimension. The mind of the fifth dimension is filled only with love and light and we all should understand very well that there are only vibrations of love and light.

Apart from this, no other energy can go there. There is only unlimited love and unconditional love. There is no hatred, fear or comparison. Here your thinking power becomes so powerful that whatever you think becomes true. Here people mostly talk through telepathy.

They have the ability to read and understand each other's thoughts and feelings easily. This dimension is kind of crystalline and miraculous and you every being can have these great powers. Many times the ascended Masters come to this dimension to impart education and knowledge, to help and awaken others. It happens everywhere and at all times.

At present, not everyone on our planet Earth is able to choose for the fifth dimensional change, whether consciously or unconsciously. All souls have the option to enter this dimension i.e. whether they want to go or not. Only those who have absorbed enough light to absorb the energies of the higher dimensions there will be able to enter the fifth dimension.

Once we enter the fifth dimension we will feel that great powers have come within you. We will feel like superman. Just as you can draw infinite energies from the sun on Earth, the fifth dimension also gives us powers beyond those of ordinary humans.

Those who are on the path of ascension can fill themselves with divine vision. Their ability to see beyond material things develops. In that their third eye also gets awakened. In this they develop such abilities that they can read the minds of others. They can experience a great deal of their foresight and can absorb these experiences.

Those who have clairvoyance may also experience seeing spirits who have died or may be higher dimensional beings such as guides, divine spirits or spirits. They can also see those who are caught between earth and heaven. They may have experiences with these things that may be different, may feel different vibrations that are different from the energies of other planets.

In this way, many times we start having such experiences in life where we start getting psychic abilities. When we are walking on the path of ascent and having experiences, seeing different things, it seems as if layers are being opened from within us and curtains are being removed.

We begin to realise the multi-dimensional behaviour in our realities, our ordinary behaviour and our nature. Start going beyond it. We have the possibility of another kind of consciousness. When the level of our own consciousness starts rising, then it seems as if we are sometimes in this dimension, sometimes in some other dimension. All these things indicate to us that we are all multidimensional beings. The fifth dimension is infinite in many respects for humans who find themselves living according to universal spiritual laws. There is no place in time. They remain connected with the energies of the universe.

Many of us must have had such experiences that we are able to see the thought, see it written, like I saw meditation written, as if some pictures were written on a computer screen or canvas. People appear to us as if they are designers, artists or photographers or anyone who seems familiar to us. It helps in bringing out our inner intuition and awakening our Kundalini. When I look at a person, I can see his aura.

Some such things get activated due to which a clarity starts coming inside us. Clear feelings start coming inside us. We begin to feel the emotions of the person's soul, including feeling the pain of other people. Many people are consciously aware of this. Let's assume that whoever we meet, whether positive or negative, a strong emotion is revealed.

Whoever a person is next to us in spirit, we can tune into their emotional energy. When we are too emotional we align our emotions with the emotions of others. We heal as healers do. This ability also increases because your emotions come into play. You receive messages from the Holy God within you and you receive knowledge through different types of experiences.

All these things that are happening inside you that were not understood till now start intensifying. This is the result of the fifth dimension.

You may also feel the presence of a smell or scent that has no physical source, such as the favourite perfume of a deceased person or relative or the scent of cigarette smoke that person used. If you smell any of the Masters, the scent of sandalwood, rose, different types of smells are taking you towards the memories of your past or all of them are reminding us of our potential, through which there is a shift within us.

Similarly, there is a taste in the mouth as if a dead person is trying to connect with you. Let's say we have any food or drink item that reminds us of that person. If we have the intensity of taste then you should understand that we remember the smell of that taste and you remember the memory of your grandmother's food. Let's say we smelled a scent that instantly reminded him of you and took him to his acquaintance. In this way that person or food gives you peace and connects you with that person.

Clear cognizance means knowing clearly. When you move towards the heights, towards the fifth dimension, all these abilities within you increase. Like having a premonition. You come to know about the future and you get some information. You see it had to be this way. Miracles start happening in the fifth dimension. You start getting cured immediately, the elements within you which are divine elements, together with the divine energies, start meeting in such a vibration where you become a source of energy.

Because the vibration of God is the divine energy of love. You become a kind of medium between them, a guide. There is a love, compassion within you and then a change within you. I can tell you that when your vibration increases, such possibilities start increasing within you that you start making communication contacts many times. As this book is being written. Dialogue contact with Babaji *"Mahavatar Babaji speaks"*, here he was giving the message and I was receiving the message.

Now you must have understood well how we can talk. Humans can also speak like this in their Etheric Angelic Light Language. This thing is also possible. You get a signal in that light, in that divine love and light of God, just like in meditation I got messages in which I was told to come to a particular place, see something like this, feel something. Leave something out and see what you get.

When all this work is being done under the divine guidance of the Divine God, then change is bound to occur in life. It can be said that these divine energies of Jesus Christ, the energies of love, create within us also a divine awakening of healing and healing within our life force. When we accept this energy, this holy spirit, our soul, that divine spirit, that divine element, we feel as if we are healed. When we go through such experiences, sometimes there is a reaction in our body, sometimes we will feel cold or we will feel hot. Sometimes our hands become numb, sometimes we see some different scenes. Sometimes smoke is seen coming out from inside a person. This is all change.

The more we find motivation to increase our formal strength, the more we find that we are healing. All this happens by connecting with divine energies. All this happens because of loving healing energy. These are sacred vibrations because these energies have nothing to do with religion. You can also change your DNA while creating a more loving relationship with Divine Consciousness.

Thank you Babaji!

27 TAP SWADHYAY ESHWAR PRANIDHAN KRIYA YOGA

In my experiences with Mahavtar Babaji over the years, he has given me various messages of ascension. I would like to share with you the message that Babaji gave me in 2025.

In the land of Prayagraj, Mahakumbh was happening after 144 years. I also got the opportunity to go to Mahakumbh with my family. I had only one aim, to spread meditation. In 2012, while meditating, I received a message. I had a vision that we were spreading meditation at Kumbh Mela. When I shared this experience with Brahmarishi Patriji, he said, *"You have to do this."* With his complete support, at that time, we went to kumbh in Prayagraj in 2013. After that, I had the opportunity to visit again.

That day, after taking a holy dip in the Ganga, I experienced immense bliss. While bathing in the sacred waters of the Sangam, I felt a deep sense of peace and fulfillment.

☆☆☆

I had a strong desire that when I visit Prayagraj, I must go to the place where Yukteshwar Giri Ji had the darshan of Mahavatar Babaji. I had never been there before, but with this wish in my heart, we planned to visit that place. Fortunately, it was within walking distance from where we were staying, about 1.5 to 2 km away.

Since my main purpose at the Maha Kumbh was to spread awareness about meditation, on the same day, through divine coincidence, we also got an opportunity to teach meditation at a school. We were distributing pamphlets and promoting meditation.

After finishing the meditation session, we started walking through narrow lanes to reach our destination. The streets were extremely narrow. After walking some distance, suddenly, on my left-hand side, I saw a Hanuman temple. I have always felt a strong connection with Hanuman Ji's energy. As I passed by, I noticed something unusual, on the right side of the temple, there was a small structure that looked like an ashram or a house. It didn't appear like a typical spiritual place from the outside, but I felt an intense pull, as if something was calling me from within.

☆☆☆

I was drawn toward it and walked in. Inside, I saw a saint dressed in saffron robes. I asked him, *"May I enter?"* He agreed, and I stepped inside. I asked him,

"What is this place?" He replied, *"This is where we have spiritual gatherings and devotional singing."*

I requested him, *"May I sit here for some time and meditate?"* He permitted me, so I sat in a small hall. There was an altar with an idol and a throne-like seat, which, he explained, belonged to their revered Guru. Along with me, my two soul sisters also sat for meditation.

As soon as we started meditating, I experienced something extraordinary. I felt a luminous presence near my feet, a divine light. My subtle body bowed down in deep reverence, and I touched the feet of the Guru's presence. At that moment, the presence spoke to me, *"Are you going to the Kriya Yoga Ashram?"* I humbly nodded, *"Yes."* He said, *"Please convey my salutations to Mahavatar Babaji."* I smiled and replied, *"But in the higher realms, aren't we all already connected? You must already meet Him."*

He smiled and said, *"Yes, but still, please offer my respects."* With this beautiful experience, I opened my eyes.

The Yogi ji started showing me pictures of their Guru. I asked him, *"Do you know meditation?"* He said, *"No, I only serve in this temple and perform my rituals."* So, I asked him to close his eyes, and I guided him through meditation. Meanwhile, his 3-4 disciples joined us in meditation.

As I continued meditating, I received an inner message, a divine instruction, *"There is a water source here. Take some of this water with you."*

When I opened my eyes, I asked the saint, *"Was there ever a water source here?"*

He replied, *"No, not that I know of."*

I then asked, *"Is there a well here?"*

He said, *"Yes, there is a well, but it has dried up."*

I insisted, *"No, I have received a message that there is still water."*

The saint then mentioned that they had installed a tube well there. I requested him to allow me to collect some water.

He agreed, and we took the sacred water. We gratefully accepted this divine blessing and spent some more time at the ashram.

Interestingly, just a day before, a sacred fire ceremony (yagya) had taken place there as part of Gupt Navaratri. I could deeply feel the spiritual energy of the place. I realized that the divine consciousness itself had called me there.I strongly felt the presence of Maha Vidya Vasini. I also received a message from the temple's Guruji, asking me to convey his salutations to Babaji.

Although it was quite surprising for me, I still accepted it as it was. A thought crossed my mind, was Babaji testing me? Was he seeing if I could recognize him? Had he come in this form to deliver his own message? Even today, I cannot say for sure. But in every experience, I see Babaji's divine play.

When we arrived at the ashram, I wanted to see the sacred tree. However, there was no one there, everything was still and silent. Someone told us that the tree was located at Gate No. 3, but it was locked, and we couldn't see it. This filled me with disappointment. Even the tree was locked away, and I could not behold it.

As I dwelled on these thoughts, my consciousness turned inward. I chose a quiet place to sit and meditate. I observed the surroundings, and right in front of me, inscribed above the door or on a nearby wall, were the words, *"Tapah Swadhyaya Ishwarapranidhana Kriya Yogaha."* My eyes closed naturally, and I heard Babaji's voice.

He asked, *"Did you come to see the tree?"*

I replied, *"Yes, Babaji."*

He then asked, *"What would you gain from seeing that tree?"*

I answered, *"This is the place where Yukteshwar Giri Ji had your divine darshan."*

He asked, *"So, just seeing that place, what impact might it have?"*

I replied, *"I wanted to sit in that very spot and meditate, just as he had done when he received your darshan. Perhaps I, too, would have an experience in this Kumbh."*

Babaji responded, *"Have I not already given you my darshan? Have I not met you before?"*

I bowed my head and replied, *"Yes, Babaji. You have met me many times. You have blessed me with your presence countless times. Your divine consciousness has showered its grace upon me again and again."*

He smiled and asked, *"Do you remember that place? The trees around it? The air, the clouds?"*

I fell silent. These memories, what use were they to me? Perhaps, for others, they were a symbol. Just a symbol that turns into history.

Babaji then said, *"When people read and hear about your experiences, they will connect with you. That is the true essence of all this."*

I shared another experience with Babaji, *"While coming here, I felt a presence at a certain spot. Someone appeared before me and asked me to bow in reverence."* At that moment, I felt as if he was smiling and conveying something profound.

Sitting in that sacred space, I reflected deeply. I understood the meaning of Tapah, the discipline of the body, the purification of the mind, and the control over the senses. It is through tapah that one refines oneself, and one gains mastery over the senses.

Then, I contemplated Swadhyaya, the study of the self. Spiritual study is the exploration of the soul. Who am I? What is my origin? What is my end? What do I take with me? What do I leave behind? What truly belongs to me, and what is transient? Is this world dualistic, or is it non-dual? Swadhyaya means understanding all of this.

The intellect, which constantly wavers between different directions, begins to comprehend all knowledge. When it turns inward and truly perceives itself, it realizes its insignificance in the vast expanse of the universe. At that moment, all ego dissolves. By setting aside the intellect, which cannot grasp the ultimate truth, and surrendering completely to the Divine, one transcends the limitations of the mind. This process of surrender takes lifetimes for many, and when it finally happens, it marks the true beginning of Kriya Yoga.

Kriya Yoga is the yoga of action, where *"Yoga"* means union and *"Kriya"* means action. It is the state of becoming one with the breath, merging with each incoming and outgoing breath. When every action, every deed is performed in a state of surrender, it ceases to be mere action and transforms into selfless service. It is an action in which the doer disappears, where one becomes a mere witness, observing life as it unfolds. This is the essence of Kriya Yoga, as Mahavatar Babaji intends to reveal in 2025 and the times ahead.

For me, it was a profound realization that Babaji never instructed me to follow the traditional methods of yoga from the past. Instead, he said, *"That was the practice of a different time. Now, the vibrations of the Earth have risen significantly."*

The practice today is simply to sit with awareness of the breath, aligning the body with ease, merging with each inhalation and exhalation. In doing so, the mind becomes still, the intellect surrenders, and one attains self-realization. In that state, we realize, I am not this body. I am not this mind. I am not even this intellect. I am beyond all of it. I am the soul. With the awakening of the soul, every action transforms into selfless service.

Through this book, *Mahavatar babaji speaks,* I conclude my writing, hoping that these messages lead you to a place of pure and unconditional love. What could be a higher vibration than this? Love for all. Compassion for all. One action, one service. We are all one. The entire Earth is one family.

Thank you Babaji!

क्रियायोग
हं
क्षं
प्रभु ईसा मसीह

28 BREATH MEDITATION

Breath Meditation is to direct one's total attention and awareness only on one's normal, atural breathing process.

My dear readers, you all definitely want to know how I was able to converse with Babaji.

I am mentioning that Babaji used to speak, and I used to listen. How was it possible that Babaji's words were so clear to my ears? What kind of meditation practice did I follow? What kind of spiritual discipline did I undertake that enabled me to hear Babaji, feel his presence, and even see him? I want to share that method with you all.

This is called Breath Meditation.

The key is to be aware of your breath—your incoming breath and outgoing breath.

There is no need to make an effort to stop the external disturbances. Simply observe the natural flow of your breath. Gradually, withdraw your life force from the external senses and turn inward. Focus on the rhythmic movement of your breath—incoming breath, outgoing breath, incoming breath, outgoing breath.

This is the essence of Breath Meditation.

In Breath Meditation, attention of the mind should constantly be on the normal, natural breath. The task on hand is effortful, joyful oneness with the breath.

No *'mantra'* is to be chanted… no form of any *'deity'* is to be entertained in the mind… no hathayogic pranayama practices like *'kumbhaka'*… holding the breath… should be attempted.

Any comfortable sitting posture can be taken. The posture should be as comfortable as possible. Hands should be clasped and all finger should go into all fingers. Eyes should be closed.

When we are with the breath-energy, the mind becomes rather empty. Then, there is a tremendous in-flow of cosmic energy into the physical body. Gradually, the hitherto dormant third-eye begin to become activated. And, by and by, cosmic consciousness gets to be experienced.

Any comfortable sitting posture can be taken… The posture should be as comfortable as possible… It is not at all necessary that we should squat on the ground...You can perfectly prefer a comfortable sofa...

Hands should be clasped and all fingers should go into all fingers

The feet should be crossed

The eyes should be closed

Observe the normal natural breath

What happens when we meditate with the Breath Energy?

"When we are with the breath-energy, the mind becomes rather empty.

Then, there is a tremendous in-flow of cosmic energy into the physical body.

Gradually, the hitherto dormant Third-eye begins to become activated. And, by and by, cosmic consciousness gets to be experienced.

Energy Body is the structure for the Consciousness. Energy Body forms with more than 72000 Nadis or Energy tubes which run all across the Body. All these Energy Tubes starts from the head region. This region is called 'BramhaRandra'. Meditation is the journey of our consciousness towards the Self.

Sleep is unconscious Meditation. Meditation is conscious sleep. We receive some amount of Cosmic Energy in sleep and in deep silence. We receive abundant Cosmic Energy in Meditation. Meditation is the journey of our consciousness from: Body to Mind, Mind to Intellect, Intellect to Self and Beyond.

Thank you Babaji!

29 BABA MUDRA

The *"Baba Mudra"* has the ring finger and middle finger folded by the thumb finger. The two fingers that are not touched are the little finger and the index finger.

The significance is that there is that there is no need at all to tamper with the physical body in our spiritual endeavour! We should never trouble the physical body.

The physical body, in itself, is absolutely glorious and wonderful and is a pinnacle achievement of the Nature which is guided by the Nature Spirits.

No need to practice difficult Hatha Yoga Kriyas!

No need of impossible Sheersha Asanas!

The second finger — the ring finger, which represents the mind must be controlled. The Mind must be thoroughly disciplined, and should be totally rectified.

All the prejudices and stupidities of the Society are reflected truly in the Individual Mind. Such prejudices and stupidities of the Society hamper an individual's sanity and spiritual intelligence. Liquidating the impact all the prejudices and stupidities of the Society on an individual's mind is the process of meditation.

What can tame the Mind? The Cosmic Self! However, that should be 'agreed upon' by the Individual Self.

When the Individual Self wants to see that it's mind needs to be rectified and purified, it goes into meditation. Then, the Cosmic Self takes over, purifies and rectifies the Mind by means of its Cosmic Energy / Cosmic Mind.

This is the symbolic meaning of the Ring Finger being controlled by the Thumb Finger in the "Baba Mudra".

Similarly, the limited Intelligence, i.e. the Middle Finger, also, needs to be tamed because the limited worldly Intelligence represents "half knowledge" and half Knowledge is absolutely dangerous!

Half Knowledge is rectified only by Full Knowledge! And, Cosmic Self alone is Full Knowledge!

This is the symbolic meaning of the Middle Finger being controlled by Thumb Finger in the "Baba Mudra"!

When the Individual Self 'decides' to become enlightened, it chooses to go into meditation.

When the individual self chooses meditation, then, the Cosmic Self takes over and transforms the limited Intelligence (the worldly Intelligence) with its spiritual Intelligence and spiritual Knowledge also called as "Buddhi."

Transformation of "Worldly Intelligence" into *"Buddhi"* also called as *"Spiritual Intelligence"* is called as Jnana Yoga!

The most important thing to understand is that Jnana Yoga happens automatically and naturally in Dhyana Yoga.

"Baba Mudra"

Essence of "Baba Mudra"

ring finger rectified = Dhyana Yoga middle finger rectified = Jnana Yoga

Travelling from a state of "The Mind"
to a state of *"The Buddhi"* that is called as
Meditation, or Spirituality or Spiritual Science, or Enlightenment!

(By- Brahmarishi Subhash Patriji)

Thank you Babaji!

GUIDED MEDITATIONS

FULL SOUL INTEGRATION

We will do this process safely in the presence of Mahavatar Babaji.

Inhale…Exhale…

Inhale…Exhale…

Inhale…Exhale…

You keep doing it as I am telling you. I am a living soul.

I am born on earth at this time.

If any part of my consciousness, at any time, is associated with any person, any place, any event… I command it to return to my aura, to my consciousness, at this very moment.

I command myself that I am becoming a complete consciousness.

Anywhere in this lifetime of mine, if any part of my consciousness is incomplete with me, I am inviting that part to come back into my body right now.

Now you will just calm down, feel it and see it all coming back to you.

Knowingly or unknowingly, whatever part of me, emotional or otherwise, is with anyone, anywhere, is coming back into me.

What is mine, only mine, is coming to me… Coming inside me, coming inside me…

It is flowing its place in my body, in my consciousness, in my aura.

Only my own energy is coming back into my body, in all my chakras, in every layer of my chakras.

In every molecule of my body in every inch and every layer of my body, in every inch and every layer of my consciousness.

If I have someone else's, any other person's, any energy, in any form, in the form of a fragrance, in the form of a shadow, or in any other form, at this very moment it is leaving me, my body, my consciousness, my aura.

I am leaving it, it is going back, and whatever place it belongs to is going back there. Whatever is its place in the universe, it is going back there. Now quickly make a purple circle around your body. You are completely safe in this circle.

Now make another golden circle outside the purple circle.

Make another golden circle outside it. Now make another red circle outside it.

Now I am completely safe and my energy has returned to my body and my consciousness today.

Thanking all the energies, slowly open your eyes. We will do this process feeling the presence of

Mahavatar Babaji.

This is the process that Babaji told me to share with everyone.

Everyone has to do this process.

Thank you Babaji!

OPENING YOUR FIFTH DIMENSIONAL PATH WITH GOLDEN ENERGIES

Sit in a comfortable position, cross your legs, clasp your hands and close your eyes.

Take a deep breath—so deep that it reaches the Sacral Chakra and hold your breath for 5 seconds and then release it through your mouth.

Again, breath in – hold – breath out. Right now we are going with a meditation process and it is a kind of attunement. Attunement in our astral body, in our chakras and physical body too.

Again, take a deep breath. Now, bring your consciousness to your heart chakra.

Say "I am a Soul, I am a Divine Soul, I am a Divine."

The moment you are saying that you are Divine, feel your heart beating.

If you have seen any of your old self, any past life or your higher self or if you have found your Guardian Angel or if you have any Archangel with whom you connect, and then feel like that they are here with you.

Again, say it to yourself, *"I am a Divine Soul. My consciousness has been connected to my Masters, My Guru, Archangel, and Animal Guides."*

You are feeling deep peace and their vibrations in your heart. Now, feel in your heart area that a golden light is being created at that place.

The Golden Light is vibrating. Feel that Golden Light is emanating from the walls of your room, masters and from your heart.

We all are multidimensional beings. Now imagine that you are sitting in a ship and moving towards the sun at high speed, crossing the clouds, the sky, and the space.

You are going at a very high speed.

You are crossing different dimensions and moving towards the sun.

You have come close to the sun and can see the golden light. Now you are going inside the sun. It is not at all true that sun gives warmth.

Its rays and light are pleasing to you. Now move in further, you will see that as you go inside the sun, you are feeling better.

You can see some different shapes, signs or symbols over there.

You are feeling that as if there are many people around you who are your own people, you can feel them. Maybe you will find someone who is your own or belongs to your family.

Go further inside, far away there is a huge and very bright Golden Pyramid and you are moving towards the pyramid.

There is a Golden Pyramid within the sun and you within it. Look what's inside?

Many golden shapes, symbols and signs are making their presence felt.

Look carefully, what is it becoming?

Are there any Golden Dragons, Golden Dolphins or Golden Unicorns there?

Who is present?

Look at the walls of that pyramid, there is something written in light language.

You focus your consciousness there and see if it tells you something.

Say to yourself, *"I am ready to receive whatever they are trying to tell me at this time or whatever wisdom they wish to give me."*

If you are able to see any sign, shape or symbol there, then keep your right hand on it.

Now, whatever is happening in side you, allow it to unfold. Say, *"I allow myself to receive the attunement from this and I am ready for this attunement."*

Whatever is going inside you, be it any symbol, sign or shape, accept it. It is flowing through your body, bringing changes to your DNA.

Allow it to happen.

Say, *"I am ready for the change. Whatever changes are happening in my chakras, cellular bodies, and other bodies at this time, I am ready for this change.*

It is happening for my betterment and for the shift to higher consciousness, and I am ready for that."

Now you can remove your right hand.

Now look ahead and move forward. If you are able to see the Golden dragon, then look at it, otherwise, you can imagine it.

There is a Golden dragon, its tongue and body both glowing in golden colour.

You and the dragon are looking at each other. Now you will take a jump and sit on its neck.

The golden dimension energy of this place, which you have to bring to Planet Earth and you are the one who is receiving this attunement for the betterment of the Planet Earth and you are ready.

The moment you sat on the dragon, it started flying and took you to the king's chamber of the golden pyramid.

Golden dust particles, through solar energy, are being shifted to the Planet Earth and are entering your body from all around.

Your body, consciousness, system, imagination, manifestation, abundance, growth, prosperity and relationships are all being filled with filled with abundant golden energy.

Look inside yourself and notice what kind of emotions are arising at this moment. How are you feeling right now after the attunement?

The attunement process is done.

If you want and if you can, see the cellular structures of your body, they have been changed.

Look at your feelings, they have been converted. You are not the same person as you were before this process.

The whole aura of your body is now golden in colour.

Now, you feel a joyful state, a dancing state, an enlightened state—enjoy it.

There is no difference left between you and the light, now, you are the light.

Now you are a golden being made up of gold and the golden vibrations that are the highest vibrations.

Now you are going to bring these vibrations back to the Planet Earth.

Now, it is time for you to be grateful.

Be thankful for the divine energies of this place and all the miraculous energies.

After thanking everyone, come out of the golden pyramid and the sun. Return to your place in the same way you went there. Be aware of your physical existence and your breath. Be conscious of the incoming and outgoing breaths.

Feel your presence in the room and in your physical body, carrying the wonderful experience of this meditation.

Be aware of your incoming and outgoing breath. 5…4…3…2…1…0. Slowly, whenever you feel comfortable, you can come out of meditation, bringing with you the divine abilities that have entered within you.

Now, both your hands place them over your eyes, then slowly open your eyes.

Thank you Babaji!

EXPANDING THE CONSCIOUSNESS

Sit in a comfortable position, cross your legs, clasp your hands and close your eyes. Take a deep breath in and a deep breath out.

As you are breathing in you are receiving lots of energies, which are able to clean your different bodies, and as you are blowing out you are ready to release and cleanse your own energy place.

So, breathe in and breathe out three times to make your body relax. Be aware of your body and make yourself comfortable.

You are relaxing, starting from your toes. The muscles in your toes are relaxing.

Now, the muscles in your knees and thighs are also relaxing. You are focusing on your left side, and the muscles in your lower left abdomen are relaxing.

Your chest muscles are relaxing … relax… relaxed.

Your shoulder muscles are relaxing...relax.. relaxed.

Now, your neck muscles, facial muscles, head muscles, and even your eyebrow muscles are completely relaxed.

You are doing a long meditation.

Now, focus on the right posture as the right side of your body relaxes.

Your brain, eyes, ears, neck, shoulders, and right hand are loosening.

The chest area, upper chest, upper abdomen, and lower abdomen are becoming more relaxed.

Your eyes, cheeks, and feet are at ease. Now, your entire body is completely relaxed.

Stay with your breath, each and every cell in your body is relaxing.

Your physical body is now fully at ease and in a state of deep relaxation.

Be aware of your breath, its normal and natural. Simply breathe in breathe out.

Now say, *"I am totally protected.*

"I am connected to Mother Earth, and I am not just a body. Right now, I am receiving energies from Mother Earth.

My body is absorbing these energies, and they are cleansing the chakras of my lower body.

"Now, I am ready to receive detox energies to clear my emotional body.

"I recognize that there are many energies within me that are holding me back.

"So, I am commanding my emotional body to focus on those points, situations, friends, or relatives—whether from this lifetime or any other.

"I allow my body and these detox energies to clear old patterns and memories that no longer serve me.... I am releasing these energies in these moments.

"I forgive everyone. I have now become a part of this flow. Now, I can work on releasing, one by one, whatever no longer serves me."

Release… Release…

You can imagine yourself in a water body, simply letting go. As you flow with the water, you release all those old memories.

Whatever no longer serves you.

May be problems, situations, or emotions, Let it all go.

It's okay, it's okay—no complaints. Energies are helping me.

Now, it's time to Say *"Thank you so much for coming into my life, you have given me so much. I have no complaints, no judgments. I am truly grateful. Sending you lots of love.*

As we take a turn and release these energies. *"I'm sorry if I have ever hurt you. Please forgive me."*

Imagine that the person is forgiving you in the presence of these beautiful detox energies and both of you are expressing your gratitude to each other.

You are sending lots of love to them and it is the time to release the old patterns, memories and energies. Your emotional body is becoming more clear, brighter, sharper, and powerful.

At the same time, you are inviting more people, whoever they may be from this lifetime, welcome them.

Say, *"Thank you so much, my soul brothers and sisters, my physical brothers and sisters, and my dear family. Thank you from the bottom of my heart. I am truly grateful for the wonderful bond that we share. I have learned so much from you all. But now, it is time to release—no complaints and no judgments. I am ready to move on in a different direction. It is time to let go. Thank you so much."*

Send lots of love to all of them and release...

You are feeling very light, clear and your chest area is becoming more brighter and richer. Your inner bodies are filled with very vibrant energies. If you are feeling something else around your emotional body or anything is left, imagine violet light and request them to clear your space.

Be aware of your incoming and outgoing breath. 5...4…3...2…1…0. Rub both your hands together and place them gently over your eyes and with a smile on your face, slowly open your eyes.

Thank you Babaji!

ACTIVATING YOUR LIGHT CODES

Sit in a comfortable position, cross your legs, clasp your hands and close your eyes. Bring your awareness to your breath. You are going to work on your Sacral Chakra.

Inhale deeply… and exhale…

Inhale deeply… and exhale…

Inhale deeply… and exhale…

Now, direct your awareness towards your second chakra. Even if you cannot see it, tell yourself, "I am balancing my Sacral Chakra, it is coming into alignment, in the presence of Mahavatar Babaji and with the blessings of my guru."

Visualize yourself as a new-born baby.

Imagine, if you can, or simply recall the memory of your birth.

You have just entered this world, a tiny infant, a new-born, a fresh soul that has arrived on this Earth. Now, take this new-born baby into your heart center.

You can do it, yes, you can. Take your consciousness and place the baby within your Heart Chakra, a tiny child resting inside your heart.

"I have come into this birth as an infant. I have taken birth many –many times. I have come to this Earth many times. In those countless births, I have formed many relationships as parents, husband and wife, children, and friends. My connection with this world has been created over and over again."

You are now going deeper and deeper.

You have taken birth in many countries, many times.

Your soul is one, but you have taken different bodies, sometimes as a woman or a man.

Sometimes in another civilization or another era. Yet, you are one soul. In all these births, your Sacral Chakra has accumulated memories, experiences, and karmic impressions.

These memories repeat, again and again, and still, something remains, something is left behind. But today, in this lifetime, in this form, with the help of your Sacral Chakra, your Guru, your Masters, and your Spirit Guides, you will go within, you will understand, and you will destroy and eliminate what no longer serves you.

Now, visualize in front of you a tiny point of light, a small dot of light appearing before you. As it comes closer, it grows larger. This light is your Masters, who have arrived to help you.

Focus on the light and follow it like a torch guiding your way. Suddenly, the light grows wings, and with its wings, you too begin to fly.

You are rising higher and higher, traveling deep within your heart's core, passing through a tunnel. Crossing through a passageway.

This journey is to discover your true existence. Now, you are being taken to a place where higher beings, enlightened masters, and luminous souls reside, ready to assist you. You have reached this sacred space. Now, pause and observe. Look around. You can see your Masters standing before you. Even if you cannot see them, know that they are giving you a weapon.

Look at what weapon you have received.

It could be a trident (trishaw), a sword, a dagger, or anything else. Every one of you has received a weapon.

Now, from this higher place, turn your attention towards your Sacral Chakra.

Just focus on your Sacral Chakra. Using this weapon, take the name of your Guru and begin to dig around your Sacral Chakra.

Keep digging, dig deeper and deeper. Just like removing old soil to plant a new seed, dig further.. go deeper.

If you find anything rotten, decayed, or useless, remove it. Take it out of your body, out of your Sacral Chakra.

These old burdens are blocking your progress. If you see anything that no longer serves you, remove it, clean that space completely.

Now, place a beautiful Golden Merkaba (a six-pointed geometric energy field) at this spot. Fill this space with Compassionate Energy be it pink, orange, or any colour energy that resonates with you. Now, meditate on this space for five minutes. This is your Sacral Chakra.

Now, observe the Merkaba Energy rising from your Sacral Chakra.

This energy is now spreading through all the cells of your body.

It is moving upward, flowing freely. Say, "I am a soul. I have come to fulfil my divine purpose on this Earth."

Each cell in your body is filling with Merkaba Energy.

You can visualize a white light or a rainbow light spreading. If your Guru, Masters, Spirit Guides, the Divine, or the Holy Spirit have given you a sacred symbol… you may use that too.

Now, fill your entire body with this light. From head to toe, let this energy radiate outward.

Observe how your energy is expanding beyond your physical body, sending out light to the world. You are radiating peace, joy, and bliss.

Now, you are preparing your portal.

You are placing a Heart Energy Tower, launching a satellite of consciousness from your Sacral Chakra.

Visualize a pink pyramid, a Rose Quartz energy field arriving at your physical space.

Place it there. See your Guru. If they have a message for you, receive it now.

You are now fully prepared for Earth's healing, physical and subtle service.

Now, you are returning from this place. The Masters take back the weapon they gave you.

You offer your gratitude.

Take a moment to look around once more.

Now, see your entire existence from this higher perspective. Feel your chakras coming into perfect balance. Once again, the light appears before you.

With the guidance of this light, you now return through the tunnel, returning to your Heart Centre. The new-born child, the light within you.

You thank this light as it departs.

Now, the new-born baby returns to your Sacral Chakra. Your memory is fading. You are coming back to your present state.

Say, "Today, I am understanding the Seven Spiritual Bodies. I am realizing my own soul through inner rebirth. I am not the body. I am not the mind. I have different bodies, but I am one Supreme Soul. I bow to my true self. I bow to my divine form."

You express gratitude to all energies, to everyone who guided this process, to Mother Earth, for preparing you for service. You are now ready for both physical and spiritual service.

Take a deep breath in and a deep breath out.

No thoughts, no mind, just stillness.

Those who received guidance from animal spirits, chakras, divine light, colours, higher masters, deities, and 5D energy, express gratitude.

This transformation is eternal.

Have complete faith.

Relax… completely relax.

5... 4... 3... 2... 1.

Rub both your hands together and place them gently over your eyes and with a smile on your face, slowly open your eyes.

Emerge from this profound meditation.

If you wish to stay, remain as long as you like. It is so profound.

Thank you Mahavatar Babaji!

Thank you Ascended Masters!

ABOUT THE AUTHOR

AshaShri is a spiritual scientist, pyramidologist, author, artist, and a public speaker. She has been on a spiritual journey since 1975.Her parents were Shri Surender Kumar Bansal and Pramda Bansal. They gave her Physical name Asha .

Asha Shri felt the unmistakable presence of divinity around her from early childhood. She grew up listening to the stories of Gargi and Maitreyi, and aspired to be like them. Her curious mind had questions, prime among them being about life after death, which largely remained unanswered.

She tried scouting for them in religious texts, the Vedas, Upanishads and scriptures, and during this pursuit she got deeply acquainted with the Gayatri

Mantra-one of the most powerful chants to the Divine Mother. She began chanting this mantra and performed several Mahayagnas (rituals) using this mantra. Her pursuits were supported by her first Guru Ram Sharma Acharyaji. She worked as a social worker with Shrimati Lt Sarla Mudgalji from 1976 to 1980, for Women Welfare – Women Empowerment as Beti Bachao, Dowry etc. Regarding these awakening, she met with our Late Prime Minister Indira Gandhiji and President Shri Giani Jail Singh Ji.

Asha is married with her soulmate Arun Kumar Gupta and continued their Spiritual journey with their daughter Devika Gupta and son in law Devanshu Chaudhary.

Her life took another turn in 1994 when she met Pramila Bhagwan who answered her lingering questions much to her satisfaction. With her blessings she went through an inner transmutation which awakened an intimate connection with her Soul. Then she devoted her life to the service of spreading knowledge.

Since 2010, she has been associated with the Pyramid Spiritual Societies Movement (PSSM) under the guidance of the PSSM's founder, Brahmarshi Patriji. In the year 2010, she connected with the higher realms and was guided by Mahavatar Babaji for creating Paradise on Planet Earth.

Asha Gupta devotes much time to meditation and helps those who come to her to learn meditation. Her spiritual work is enthused by veganism, meditation, and the power of the pyramid and crystals. She also has knowledge of designing, counselling, mandala art, breathing, and hypnosis.

She received the *"Make in India"* award in 2017 for her contribution to spreading the knowledge of pyramids at the PHD Chamber of Commerce, Delhi. She has to her credit several translations of spiritual books and author of many books such as *"Anapanasati Meditation", "New Age Pyramid Energy"* and *"Yogi Bhavarjun"*.

Serving her purpose, Asha Gupta received the honorable title of *"Brahmavidwanmani"* in the year 2018.She is honoured by *"Honorary Doctrate"* and *"Life Time Achievement Award"* in 2022.

She is the founder of Awakening Beyond and Pyramid Light, the purpose of which was to spread the light of Pyramid Energy and New Age Spiritual Evolution. Both are a unit of Asha Foundation.

In the year 2020, again she connected with the higher realms and was guided by Mahavatar Babaji and Aadi Shakti to create ripples of Divine Feminine Energy across India. Her dedication to awakening the divine feminine also led to the establishment of 'White Sisterhood' for the world.

Her divine expedition led her to start a 365 days initiative of *'Global Peace and Vegetarianism'* in 2021, with the purpose of creating energies of peace and harmony on our beloved planet.

Since 2023, she has been leading the Adishakti Dhyan Yatra across various parts of the world, including Australia, Philippines, Thailand, J&K, Gujarat,Rajasthan and many more. Through this spiritual journey, she continues to spread the profound practice of meditation, empowering individuals to connect with their inner selves and experience deeper states of peace and awareness.

Brahmavidwanmani Asha Gupta has enabled more than 5,00,000 school students, working professionals and individuals on the path of Breath Meditation, over the last 15 years. Her mission is to teach meditation to 1 crore students, guiding them toward inner peace and self-awareness.

She is the founder of a spiritual School named *"Global School of Rising Stars"* (GSRS) which is a spiritual school, with an innovative approach to nourish the uniqueness in students and enable young talents to position themselves best in different walks of life. Along with regular studies, GSRS helps students to develop their characters and minds, and prepares them to live peaceful and successful life. Its aim is to stimulate the divine potential inherent in children through fun-filled activities, and equip them with the tools they need to deal with this tough world. The institute offers free classes to kids aged 4-15.

Asha Gupta's life and work are a true testament to the power of spiritual dedication and transformation. Her vision of '*Vasudhaiva Kutumbakam*'—which means 'the world is one family', reflects the idea that all beings, including plants, animals, and humans, are interconnected.

She believes that the divine resides in every being and promotes love, peace, and harmony. Through wisdom and meditation, she inspires individuals to know themselves. Her work continues to ignite a New Age spiritual revolution, grounded in unity and transformation.

Connect with us:

Website - ashafoundationadishakti.com

Facebook - pyramidlight1

Youtube - ashafoundation-AdiShakti

Instagram - asha.pyramidlight

Author Books

www.ingramcontent.com/pod-product-compliance
Ingram Content Group UK Ltd.
Pitfield, Milton Keynes, MK11 3LW, UK
UKHW041828200726
13854UKWH00002BA/652